SPEEDWAY
THE CLASSIC ERA

SPEEDWAY
THE CLASSIC ERA

Philip Dalling

HALSGROVE

First published in Great Britain in 2011
Reprinted 2014

British Library Cataloguing-in-Publication Data
A CIP record for this title is available from the British Library

ISBN 978 0 85704 104 3

HALSGROVE
Halsgrove House,
Ryelands Business Park,
Bagley Road, Wellington, Somerset TA21 9PZ
Tel: 01823 653777   Fax: 01823 216796
email: sales@halsgrove.com

Part of the Halsgrove group of companies
Information on all Halsgrove titles is available at: www.halsgrove.com

Printed and bound in China by Everbest Printing Co Ltd

CONTENTS

ACKNOWLEDGEMENTS

T HIS, MY third speedway book is, like its predecessors, essentially a tribute to the skill and bravery of the riders who year-in and year-out thrill and entertain crowds the length and breadth of Great Britain and across the globe.

Once again, its preparation has involved the pleasurable task of seeking out and interviewing a great many former riders and promoters (and members of their immediate families), in this country and overseas. Their unfailing courtesy is matched only by the sharpness of their memories and for this I am very grateful.

Personal recollections of the period covered by *SPEEDWAY The Classic Era* – essentially the first 40 years of the sport's existence in Britain, from the late 1920s to the late 1960s – photographs, press cuttings, mementoes, advice and assistance of various kinds have been provided by the following:

Bob Andrews, Harry Bastable, Geoff Bennett, Victoria Bennett, Jim Bond, Janet Bond, Eric Boocock, Erol Brook, Peter Brough, Barry Briggs, Raymond 'Buster' Brown, the late Ivor Brown, John Carpenter, Howard Cole, Lew Coffin, Ted Connor, Mavis Connor, Ray Cresp, Ray Day, Danny Dunton, Reg Duval, Reg Fearman, Ove Fundin, Peter Gay, Fred Greenwell, Lou Grepp, John Hart, Pat Hart, Barbara Hart, Clive Hitch, Eric Hockaday, Ian Hoskins, John Jones, Harold Lander, Sara Allsopp Lander, the late Louis Lawson, Hilda Lawson, Ivan Mauger, Ken Mellor, Leo McAuliffe, Ernest Palmer, the late Norah Palmer, Irene Palmer, John Pilblad, Graham Plant, Colin Pratt, Norman Redmond, John Reason, Tony Robinson, Doreen Robinson, Cyril Roger, Eric 'Bluey' Scott, Len Silver, Colin Smith, Francesca Stadelmayr, Terry Stone, Ken Vale, Keith Whipp, Vic White, Fred Williams, Ray Wilson, Peter Wrathall and June Wrathall.

My grateful thanks also go to the many fellow speedway journalists, authors, and historians, and others who love the sport, who have patiently and generously answered my many queries and also provided photographs:

Robert Bamford, Bob Bath, Brian Bott, John Chaplin, Brian Darby, Bryan Horsnell, Trevor James, John Jarvis, Alan Jones, Mike Kemp, Tony McDonald of *Classic Speedway* and *Backtrack*, Colin Parker, John Skinner, John Somerville, Barry Stephenson, Dave Stallworthy, John Stallworthy, John Sumpter, Tony Webb and Wendy Wills.

Special thanks to all of the contributors to the invaluable *Speedway Researcher* magazine and website, and in particular to Jim Henry and Graham Fraser. In addition I always look forward to Thursday evenings and a new edition of the *Speedway Plus* website.

I have again consulted a wide range of books, newspapers, magazines and programmes, particularly the books: *Speedway: The Pre-War Years* by Robert Bamford, assisted by Dave Stallworthy (Tempus*); Speedway in Manchester 1927-1945* by Trevor James and Barry Stephenson (Tempus), *Homes of British Speedway* by Robert Bamford and John Jarvis (Tempus), *Coventry's Two Speedways* by Colin Parker, *Owlerton Legends* by Matthew Jackson and Paul Rickett, (Pendragon Books), *History of the Speedway Hoskins,* by Ian Hoskins, *As Luck Would Have It: A Cockney's Tale,* by Len Silver (Retro Speedway), *The First Book of British Speedway* (Bonar Books), *Speedway in Leicester* (Alan Jones), *Speedway and Me* by Graham Warren (Speedway Echo), *The Complete Book of Speedway* by Cyril May (Haynes), *Broadside to Fame* by Leonard Sandys (Findon), *The Illustrated History of Speedway by Martin Rogers* (Studio Publications); and the magazines, journals and handbooks: *The Motorcycle, Motorcycling, Speedway News, Speedway World, Speedway Star and News, Stenners Speedway Annuals* 1946-1954, *The People Speedway Guides, Speedway Star Digest,* and *The Five Star Speedway Annual.*

I was privileged to be able to spend a memorable day looking through the Belle Vue collection held by Chetham's Library in Manchester, working at a table occupied in the past by Karl Marx, Friedrich Engels, Charles Dickens and Benjamin Franklin.

Thanks are also due to the staff of the British Newspaper Library at Colindale, Churchill College, Cambridge, and Bridget Warrington and Trevor Dunmore at the Royal Automobile Club.

My apologies to anyone inadvertently missed from this list of acknowledgments.

Speedway, of course, is not simply a subject for historical study. It is a living sport which, as I write in the early summer of 2011, has made a spirited start to its 84th season in Britain. During the period of research for this book I have been fortunate enough to be able to watch speedway in England, Scotland and Wales, with an itinerary stretching from Eastbourne on the south coast to Highbridge on the Somerset Levels, the Millennium Stadium in Cardiff, Coventry, Wolverhampton and Leicester in the midlands, Peterborough in the east of England, Belle Vue and Sheffield in the north, through to Glasgow north of the border.

Long may speedway continue as a truly nationwide and international sport and entertainment.

Very special thanks to Reg and Eileen Fearman for their support, and to Reg for reading the manuscript and making many helpful suggestions.

My speedway travels and the time spent writing this book would have been much less pleasant without the constant support and the company of Brenda Dyer, for which I am extremely grateful.

INTRODUCTION

SPEEDWAY, FOR many years not noticeably well served by literature, has seen a significant recent expansion in the number of volumes vying for the attention of fans. As the sport gets closer and closer to the centenary of its birth, interest in its past continues to grow.

A fan's bookshelves can now embrace not just the yearbooks and statistical surveys with which the sport has traditionally been well supplied, but also detailed histories of individual tracks and a wealth of rider autobiographies and biographies.

SPEEDWAY The Classic Era is essentially a look at many of the themes which shaped the sport in Britain during its first 40 years, from the late 1920s to the swinging sixties. These include the controversy over speedway's origins, the initial battle for control between motorcycle clubmen and commercial promoters, the constant cycle of boom and bust, the struggles of aspiring riders to carve out careers, especially during speedway's periods of depression, the thrills and, sadly, the spills, which over the years have cost many lives.

The choice of British speedway's first four decades as an overall theme for the book is deliberate. They truly represent the sport's classic era. Once speedway had made the transition from what was virtually a circus attraction, to a status as a serious sport/entertainment, most of the basics changed remarkably little over that period.

If you take a team group or an action shot from the late 1930s and put them alongside similar studies from the '40s, '50s, and even the early-to-mid 1960s, on the surface at least there are more similarities than differences. The first half of speedway's history essentially saw evolution, not revolution.

The late 1960s, in contrast, saw not just the start of another golden age which rivalled, if it never equalled, the late 1940s, but also represented a real tipping point. The radical changes that have taken place in the years since then have far outstripped anything that occurred earlier, changing the appearance of speedway, if not its basic form and spirit.

Riders throughout the first four decades were almost exclusively clad in black leather. After the early days when riders utilised a huge variety of motorcycles, including the famous tailored Douglas and Rudge machines, the JAP engine manufactured by the British firm of J A Prestwich, became standard, although there was always great variation in terms of frames, tyres etc, and a gulf in standards of tuning and machine preparation between individual competitors.

In the mid-1960s the JAP monopoly was broken by the Czech-manufactured ESO or

Jawa machines, opening the floodgates to continual technical innovation, prompted by not only a desire for greater speed and efficiency, but also by the need for progress in respect of safety and the environment.

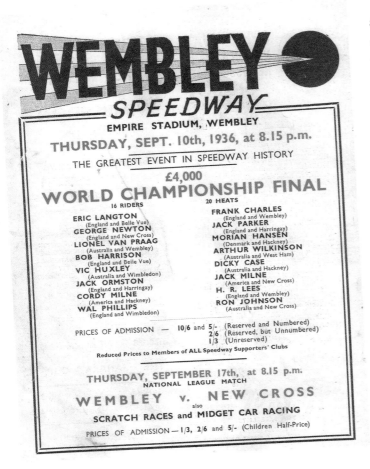

Speedway's Blue Riband event, the one-off World Championship Final, was held exclusively at Wembley Stadium between 1936 and 1960. From 1961 until 1981 the Empire Stadium shared the staging of the event with a variety of European venues, and Los Angeles in the United States. In 1995 the qualifying rounds and a one-off final were replaced by a Grand Prix system. The advertisement pictured is for the first-ever World Final in 1936 *(see Chapter Five for the background to international speedway)*.

Sponsorship was officially frowned upon during speedway's first four decades. A rider in the 1950s who painted the name of his motorcycle business on his fuel tank, was hauled before the authorities and told to explain himself.

By the early 1970s a group photograph of some of the leading riders shows them all wearing coloured leathers. Today, it is often difficult to pick out club logos from the mass of advertising stickers that cover a rider's whole body, as well as his machine.

Sponsorship, a real need as crowd levels have declined, has developed to the stage where the engine of a speedway bike is wholly covered by a protective sheet, presenting considerable additional surface areas for company insignia and names.

Match programmes, which in the past basically constituted little more than a race card, are now a major vehicle for sponsorship. Speedway's survival into the twenty-first century owes much to its ability to evolve and adapt, without losing its basic appeal.

Every fan has his or her favourite era, largely depending upon the time when they first saw the sport in action. This is true for the author, for whom the early 1960s will always have a special appeal.

Nevertheless, in the second decade of the new millennium, for myself and for thousands of others, the walk from the car park to the turnstiles, the moment when the sound of machines being warmed up in the pits first becomes apparent and, perhaps most of all, the first whiff in the nostrils of burning fuel, remains absolutely magical.

Philip Dalling
Exmoor, 2011

Chapter one

CONTROVERSIAL TO ITS CORE

Who invented speedway?

As speedway in Britain edges ever closer to its centenary, arguments over its origins intensify. Several nations claim to have been the first to stage organised motorcycle racing on loose-surfaced oval circuits, and there is more than one contender for the title of Father of Speedway. *Although he may not have been the sole originator of the activity that eventually became the sport as it is recognised today, one man, New Zealand-born John Stark Hoskins, has the greatest claim of all to the coveted title.*

A forerunner to speedway in the north west. Belle Vue in Manchester staged a historic floodlit grass-track meeting in May 1928, on what was to become the site of the famous Hyde Road speedway stadium.

SPEEDWAY THRIVES on controversy. There can be no other rational explanation for how a sport which has threatened to tear itself apart on so many occasions has survived for so long.

Eternal disputes between international governing bodies and their national counterparts, between national administrators and individual club promoters, between promoters and riders, not to mention clashes between the authorities and fans annoyed

Dirt track racing on a trotting track at Greenford in Middlesex in 1928.

The New Zealander Johnnie Hoskins and the Australian A J Hunting may dispute between themselves the title of Father of Speedway. The prime English candidate for such an honour would undoubtedly be Lionel Wills, whose championing in the British motorcycle press of the racing he had seen in Australia inspired clubs to stage the sport for themselves. Wills was a rider too, and is seen (left) with Australian test star Ron Johnson at Crystal Palace, in a study that illustrates the push starts of speedway's earliest days.

by frequent rule changes, can be a source of intense irritation or wry amusement, depending where you stand.

If you are a promoter trying to turn a profit or merely attempting to keep their head above water, a rider simply wanting to get out on the track, race and earn a living, or a fan who just wants to watch his or her team in action, the in-fighting is an irritant, to say the least. To those on the sidelines, including the media, it is all faintly amusing, causing shoulders to be shrugged as if to say, 'well, that's speedway for you.'

During the winter of 2010-2011 there appeared to be a strong possibility that two of the sport's most prominent and prestigious club sides, Coventry *Bees* and Peterborough *Panthers*, would be excluded from the top tier of league racing in Britain, the Elite League.

The annual row over regulations for each new season had, on this occasion, been even fiercer than usual. At a meeting of the British Speedway Promoters Association, the

The spectacle of speedway or dirt-track racing in its infancy. Wilfred Spencer Lamont, better known as 'Cyclone Billy' Lamont, one of the Australian pioneers, demonstrates the art of broadsiding at speed, using the leg-trailing technique of the pre-war era, around a deep cinder circuit, on his high-framed AJS machine.

representatives of Coventry and Peterborough allegedly walked out. As a result, they were deemed to have left the Elite League of their own accord. Plans were made to run the 2011 season without them, to the horror not only of their own loyal fans but to the dismay of most people who had the best interests of the sport at heart.

Coventry, an ever-present side in British speedway since 1948, were the ruling champions of the Elite League and Peterborough, with a 40-year record of existence, were another most significant outfit. It was as though Manchester United and Arsenal had been effectively expelled from the football Premiership, because of a relatively minor disagreement over rules.

The fans of the two clubs, and many neutral observers, endured a difficult winter, until at the very last minute, there was a peace deal and Coventry and Peterborough were restored to their Elite status.

A journalist with some knowledge of speedway might well have said that such an outcome was utterly predictable, given the sport's track record (no pun intended). Despite the discomfort for the supporters of both teams, most people in speedway probably expected everything to come right in the end.

Given the fact that bitter disputes are a part of the modern sport, it is no surprise that the very origins of speedway are the subject of considerable wrangling.

Rugby football is faithful to the memory of William Webb Ellis, who with a fine disregard for whatever rules existed in the mid-nineteenth century at his midlands public school, picked up the ball and ran. Cricket honours the memory of William Lord, the entrepreneur who established the ground that cricketers throughout the world acknowledge as the game's spiritual headquarters. Lord is rightly venerated, although cricket as a sport pre-dated his involvement by a good while.

John Stark Hoskins (1892-1987), may not have 'invented' speedway but there is undoubtedly a direct link between the meetings he organised at West Maitland, New South Wales, Australia, in the mid-1920s and the sport as it exists today.

The riders from Australia, New Zealand, the United States and elsewhere who flocked to Britain in 1928 not only thrilled the crowds with their own performances but acted as tutors to the aspiring home stars. Stewie St George, pictured here, was one of the overseas stars who also acted as a consultant, advising on the construction of the countless new tracks that were built across the UK. These were established in a wide variety of venues from the Olympic Stadium at the White City in London to the Thrum Hall cricket ground in Halifax.

Speedway legends 1. Australian star Vic Huxley (left) takes an outside line against England's Jack Parker. Huxley, born in Brisbane, was an instant superstar upon arrival in Britain in 1928. His UK league career was based entirely in London, first with Harringay and then with Wimbledon. He captained Australia in 26 out of his 34 test appearances. Parker, who with brother Norman was initially attached to hometown team Coventry, became a true giant of the sport, racing from its birth in Britain until 1954.

Many venues which later saw bona-fide speedway at the highest level began by staging grass-track racing on oval circuits. This is Nottingham, known as the Olympic Speedway even before a cinder surface was laid to replace the grass, with the pushers in action at the start of a race.

Most sports have reached a consensus about their histories. Not speedway. With rival claims to be the birthplace of short circuit motorcycle racing on a loose surface (not a bad definition of what speedway is all about) from the United States, South Africa, the Republic of Ireland and Britain, the sport is fertile soil for continuing argument.

In contrast to the unassailable status of Webb and Lord, the name and reputation of John S Hoskins, a man involved with the promotion of the sport for sixty years, while precious to perhaps a majority of speedway people (including the author) is reviled by others. In recent times there has been a systematic attempt to denigrate the man as an individual and to downgrade his role and contribution to speedway's development.

It is clearly wrong to say that Hoskins, or indeed any one individual 'invented' speedway. Men (and women) have raced motorcycles ever since two machines first found themselves going in the same direction, on the same stretch of road, at the same time.

Motorcycle racing branched off into many directions, including road racing, on actual public roads, in the Isle of Man style, or on private circuits with a hard surface, scrambling and trials riding over rough countryside, hill climbing and, closest in spirit and style to speedway, grass-track racing. All these branches proliferated in the early part of the twentieth century.

In the United States men raced on steeply-banked circuits constructed from timber boards, a particularly dangerous form of motorcycle sport, which produced frequent

Nottingham, primitive in the previous picture, developed swiftly. The large crowds pictured behind the riders on the cinder banks (note also the tramway-type lighting standards) were watching a representative match (although not an official test fixture) between England and Australia. This is the England team, l-r Billy Ellmore, Cyril 'Squib' Burton, Wally Humphrey, Frank Varey, Fred Strecker and Hal Herbert.

Spencer 'Smoky' Stratton was a pioneer New Zealand rider who became involved with promoting the sport in Britain. He was a member of the group who ran the sport at Sheffield in the late 1920s and is pictured in the pits at Owlerton Stadium in the steel city.

Honoured by Queen and Country, if not by all speedway commentators, especially in Australia. Johnnie Hoskins and his wife Audrey are pictured outside Buckingham Palace after he had been invested with the MBE.

Johnnie Hoskins' gravestone in Herne Bay, Kent, where he lived for many years. His family, and many, many speedway people had no doubt about his right to the title of Father of Speedway.

fatal casualties (among spectators as well as riders). The United States, South Africa and other nations also saw racing on loose, dirt surfaces, which have a strong claim to be counted as forerunners of speedway.

What is incontestable is the direct link between what Johnnie Hoskins began in New South Wales in the mid-1920s, and the 30 or so speedway meetings that take place in Britain each week throughout a season lasting from March to October, to say nothing of league racing in Scandinavia and central and eastern Europe, and other activity in various parts of the globe.

Hoskins, born in Waitara, New Zealand in 1892, trained as a wireless telegraphist, moved to Australia, and in World War One served in the Royal Australian Navy. Like many people after the war ended, he found himself almost at his wits end in the challenging Australia of the early 1920s. His search for a new role in life took him to West Maitland in New South Wales, reputedly after he had asked a railway booking clerk in Sydney to sell him a ticket to the value of the coins he had left in his pocket.

Eventually, he landed a job as secretary to the local agricultural society which, like Johnnie himself, was struggling financially. Hoskins convinced the society that there was money to be earned by presenting a form of motorcycle racing on the trotting track at the showground, initially as part of a carnival in December 1923.

The experiment developed into a regular attraction, drawing the crowds, and in 1925 Hoskins moved to the NSW coastal city of Newcastle, promoting the activity at a new, larger arena, where the riders included Americans with experience of similar racing at home.

So far, Johnnie Hoskins had organised the new sport on behalf of others who had made the financial investment. In 1926 he struck out on his own, but his attempts to promote at a major venue in Sydney hit trouble, when the summer proved to be wet.

Throughout his career, Johnnie Hoskins was to follow a pattern of working to make profits for others, followed by promoting on his own behalf when personal finances allowed, followed (after further financial setbacks) by returning to be a manager for other concerns. His biggest success down under came in Perth, Western Australia, where, in the words of his son Ian, 'he made a stack of money'. Married, and by now with a wife and two children, Hoskins could have settled for what he had, but his instincts were those of a gambler.

Others in Australia had noticed the appeal of dirt track, or speedway, racing. A J Hunting promoted successfully in Brisbane and, with his brother Frank, actually beat Hoskins to the punch in Britain. Hunting and his contracted Australian and American riders arrived in the UK soon after the dirt-track meeting at High Beech in Essex, promoted by a local motorcycle club, which is generally accepted as the first real presentation of the sport in this country.

The Huntings, and the company they founded with British partners, International Speedways Ltd, took dirt-track away from its rustic beginnings into some of the smartest stadia in the country, built for greyhound racing. They were initially successful, until internal disputes within the company led to their leaving Britain to promote in Argentina, eventually returning to their homeland.

It would be wrong to underestimate the role the Huntings (and others) played in the formation of speedway as a professional activity in Britain. Their part in the sport's development in the UK was, however, fleeting, and by the time the author began to take an active interest in speedway, in the early 1960s, their names were known only to fans of a certain age.

In contrast, because of the role he had played as a promoter, manager, and speedway showman supreme for so many years, Hoskins was a character familiar to the vast majority of supporters.

Speedway legends 2. Veteran promoter Johnnie Hoskins (left) shares the limelight at a reunion event with five-times World Champion Ove Fundin of Sweden.

My first meeting with J S Hoskins was in the middle '60s, when he was already well past his 70th birthday. It was his practice to act as team manager for his son Ian's Edinburgh *Monarchs* for many of the side's away matches in England, and his travels usually turned into something of a royal progress, such was the affection for the man around the tracks.

Hoskins attracted controversy throughout his long career in speedway racing, which included spells at Wembley, West Ham, Bradford, Newcastle, New Cross, and Belle Vue, Manchester. He also promoted in Scotland, often appearing in Highland dress, and the ritual of riders burning his trilby hat in the centre of the track became part of his legend.

Well into his 70s, Johnnie Hoskins enjoyed a speedway indian summer in the late 1960s and early '70s, creating a new venue in the cathedral city of Canterbury in 1968, introducing a new public to the sport and developing many young riders. He was awarded the MBE for his services to speedway and died at his home in Kent in 1987, five days before his 95th birthday.

Not everyone in speedway approved of his stunts, his mock rage, and his publicity seeking (most of the best Hoskins stories were, inevitably, told to the fullest advantage by the man himself). Speedway, like most other activities, has always had its roundheads and its cavaliers.

Son Ian, a multi-track promoter and a showman in his own right, is understandably dismissive of the attempts to sideline his father's role in speedway's birth and development. In his book *History of the Speedway Hoskins* he delivered this verdict:

> There have been repeated attempts, particularly in Australia, to deny credit to my father for pioneering the sport, claiming that other motorcycle events were staged earlier in Sydney.
>
> I do not deny this. But all the previous events petered out. There was no continuity. The straight line my father created from West Maitland, to Perth, to High Beech and to the present day, is the genuine foundation of speedway racing as we now know it.

Chapter two

SPORT OR ENTERTAINMENT?
The fight for speedway's soul

Dirt track racing, as it was invariably known in Britain in its earliest days, was initially rooted solidly in the amateur and gentlemanly world of the weekend motorcycle clubman. Many believed this should be the new sport's proper place in the scheme of things, but the large crowds attracted to meetings in Australia had demonstrated its potential to generate profits. Canny entrepreneurs from the other side of the world and their British partners soon steered the sport into sophisticated metropolitan stadia.

T HE BIKERS who gather at weekends and Bank Holidays at seaside and inland resorts across Britain are rarely fans of speedway racing. Indeed, speedway has often appeared to be almost completely divorced from other forms of motorcycle appreciation and racing, although historically many dirt-track men have been all-round competitors.

Today's bikers flock to circuits staging road racing and revere the Isle of Man TT races, with their tradition of allowing the everyday enthusiast a share of the spotlight. In contrast, they can be condescending and dismissive on the subject of speedway. Much of the disdain felt for speedway by motorcycle purists is historical. It dates back to a bitter, if short-lived dispute that produced two opposing camps immediately after the introduction of the sport to the UK.

World War One gave motorcycling a huge technological boost. In the inter-war years this translated into massive popularity for motorcycles as a means of everyday transport and the vehicle for competitive sport.

Clubs sprang up across the country, encouraging touring holidays and other social activities, and organising scrambles, trials, grass-track racing, hill climbs and other forms of competition. The organisers were drawn primarily from the ranks of the growing suburban middle class, who could afford not only to buy a machine and leathers but to take part in all the activities offered.

This activity was faithfully reported by a thriving motorcycle press, led by *Motor Cycling,* founded in 1902, and *The Motor Cycle,* which followed a year later. The magazines were only too pleased to publish the enthusiastic reports about the new dirt-track or speedway phenomenon, sent back from Australia by a variety of round-the-world travellers, including Stanley Glanfield, a Coventry motorcycle dealer who undertook a round-the-world tour on a motorcycle combination, ending up in Australia, and the wealthy Lionel Wills, men who fitted perfectly into the motorcycling establishment's preferred image of daring but gentlemanly and completely respectable adventurers.

The enthusiasm of Glanfield and Wills gave dirt-track racing a head start in Britain. The word pictures they painted of a thrilling but clean-cut activity tallied perfectly with the appetite for both speed and novelty that was such a feature of the jazz age.

The early events which are acknowledged to be part of dirt-track or speedway racing's British time-line were all organised by clubmen, anxious to put into practice the theories filtering back from Australia. The innovative Camberley and District Motor Club, founded in 1913, had been responsible in subsequent years for a huge variety of events, including motor rodeos, and motorcycle polo, in addition to the more conventional scrambles and hill climbs.

A great many of these events were organised by the club's imaginative secretary, Eric 'E O' Spence, who in 1925 accepted a new position in the north of England, which was eventually to propel him into a position of great influence in British speedway racing.

It was almost inevitable that the Camberley Club should promote some form of dirt-track racing. Although the event it staged on a patch of Surrey heathland in 1927 saw the riders racing in the opposite direction to conventional dirt-track, the right of this meeting to a place in speedway history is generally accepted.

Dirt-track racing at Droylsden, in what is now Greater Manchester, organised by the South Manchester Motorcycle Club, saw riders taking the accepted direction. Although

All roads led to the former cycle track behind the King's Oak hotel at High Beech in Essex on February 19 1928, for what is generally accepted to be the first bona fide dirt track or speedway meeting in Britain. This shot shows the view from the hotel over the pits area. The attendance was much higher than expected and, uniquely, the spectators stood on both the outside and inside of the track. Some people can clearly be seen clinging to the surrounding trees. (The John Chaplin Archive).

Action at High Beech on that momentous February Sunday in 1928, clearly showing the riders making their way through the lane of spectators, on what appears to be an extremely narrow track. (The John Chaplin Archive).

it is Camberley and Droylsden that have attracted the attention of historians since the sport's earliest days, it is likely there were other localised attempts to reproduce the Australian experience.

The spark that really ignited the wildfire growth of dirt-track racing in Britain was, again, lit by a club-based initiative.

Fired by what they had read in the specialist press about the sport in Australia, the Ilford Motorcycle and Light Car Club in Essex, affiliated to the Auto Cycle Union's Eastern Centre, applied to the ACU for a licence to stage a meeting on what had been a cycle track, behind the King's Oak pub at High Beech, near Loughton, in the same county. The application was initially rejected, on safety grounds, but the club persisted and eventually a permit was granted for Sunday February 19 1928.

True to the speedway tradition, controversy was in the air even before a wheel had been turned at High Beech. Glanfield and Wills had stimulated a lively correspondence in the columns of the motorcycle magazines, and one reader had suggested that the sport would prove unsuitable in the British climate, with the country's heavy rainfall likely to turn a circuit into 'a sea of black, glutinous mud.'

Wills was swift to reply, contending that the correspondent misunderstood the true nature of a 'dirt' track, which needed watering to lay the dust from the necessary cinder surface.

The letter from Wills appeared in *Motor Cycling* just days before the High Beech event, and proved to be excellent advance publicity for the Ilford Motor Club's initiative. Wills said:

> Road racing is a tame form of amusement compared to the cinder track and dirt-track racing has the additional advantage of being more or less weatherproof. Your readers will soon be able to prove this statement for themselves, for a number of

Australian riders and track managers will shortly be on their way to this country to help start dirt-track racing on a proper basis.

This confident last-minute endorsement of dirt-track racing by a man highly respected in the motorcycling world of the day helped to stimulate interest in the High Beech event. The interchangeable nature of the terms 'dirt-track' and speedway were illustrated by the Ilford club's own advertising, which announced 'dirt-track racing' to be staged at the King's Oak Speedway.

Jack Hill-Bailey, secretary of the Ilford Club, and his fellow officers and committee members, believed that up to 3,000 spectators might gather at High Beech. Photographs show the traditional roped-off enclosures for the pits and the parking areas familiar to anyone who has ever attended a club-based, essentially amateur motorcycle racing event. It is not difficult to conjure up images of club volunteers sitting behind a table at the entrance to the circuit, with programmes and a roll of tickets.

Some 2,000 tickets were reportedly taken along to the venue by Hill-Bailey himself, riding his own motorcycle combination, with his wife in the sidecar, clutching the 500 programmes and a cash float.

A few days after dirt-track racing's High Beech event, *Motor Cycling* devoted a page to the meeting, reporting that roads from Woodford, Walthamstow and other districts farther afield had been thronged from an early hour with vehicles making their way to the venue. The magazine reported that by lunchtime on the day the number of spectators was estimated at 12,000. The famous beech trees themselves, said the writer, 'bore a strange fruit – trousered humans perched high in the branches'.

The advance guard of the Australian invasion of the latent British dirt-track scene, promised by Lionel Wills in *Motor Cycling*, had already arrived by the first High Beech meeting, in the form of experienced riders Billy Galloway and Keith Mackay.

An early incident which brought gasps from the crowd occurred when the motor of Galloway's 500-cc overhead valve Douglas machine exploded into a mass of flames on the way to the start line. After the rider and a mechanic had pushed the bike for 50 yards or so the flames were sucked away, the engine started, and the Australian set off in pursuit of the three club riders in the heat, who had gained what seemed to be an unbeatable advantage.

Galloway and his fellow countryman were the only riders with any real experience of dirt-track racing. The magazine reported that Galloway's riding was 'of a different order altogether' and it took him just two laps to 'wriggle, in the most hair-raising manner – through the pack' and win the five lap race.

The way one of the leading enthusiast journals, *Motor Cycling*, reported the inaugural High Beech meeting a few days later.

Two speedway pioneers from contrasting backgrounds. Johnnie Hoskins (left), the entrepreneur and showman, meets up with the archetypal motorcycle clubman, Jack Hill-Bailey. (The John Chaplin Archive).

One of the biggest money earners in the earliest years of speedway was Lloyd 'Sprouts' Elder, a Californian who had travelled to ride in Australia in 1926 before moving on to England in 1928. It was reputed that he demanded – and received – an appearance fee of a minimum of £100 per meeting, in addition to any prize money, and was said to have earned the then enormous sum of £50,000 during his brief, three-year stay in the UK. He preferred the individual competition which formed the basis of speedway in its earliest period, although he raced in the Southern League for Southampton.

Motor Cycling's correspondent employed his entire repertoire of descriptive writing, recording 'hectic skids', 'violent swerves', and the 'shrieking cheers of the crowd' as the two Australians 'gambled with death in the packed arena'.

That first bona-fide dirt-track meeting also produced the first mentions of other aspects of the game familiar to speedway fans up to the present day; 'the track bordering brilliant green grass, with wreaths of blue smoke floating up and whiffs of the indescribable odour of burnt castor oil.'

The *Motor Cycling* verdict on dirt-track racing was wholly positive, if slightly lurid.

> Altogether a thoroughly exciting time; and those who love to watch mad tussles
> with death, and those to whom such strenuous fights are the very spice of life, cannot
> do better than support this dirt-track racing to the full. At the King's Oak Speedway
> all that is required is a wider course, deeper grit upon it, better protection for
> spectators and entries of riders such as we had on the day.

The rival publication, *The Motor Cycle*, was equally enthusiastic if a little more sober
in its assessment of the event, acknowledging the sport's possibilities but again placing
the emphasis on the need for a better surface, tighter safety arrangements and improved
spectator facilities.

> The Ilford Club's venture proved a great success and showed the many thousands
> who attended that the new sport has possibilities which, when fully developed,
> should result in a pastime making a wider appeal among the general public as well
> as motor cyclists.

The magazine proved prescient in its prediction that dirt-track racing would find a
wider public. It was in the area of the writer's comments on the development of the
sport that the roots of the forthcoming dispute were to be centred.

After High Beech the media interest in dirt-track racing broke out of the relatively
narrow specialist motorcycle press. On the day after the
meeting the *Daily Mirror* gave the meeting front page
coverage, setting the scene for massive public demand to
see the new sport for themselves.

The well-informed Lionel Wills had inside information
when he told magazine readers that parties from Australia,
notably A J Hunting, his brother Frank and their contracted
riders, and a smaller group headed by Johnnie Hoskins,
were on their way to Britain to help 'develop' dirt-track
racing.

'Sprouts' Elder's travels around Britain to fulfil his speedway engagements, took the form of what was effectively a royal progress. Opposing riders queued up to be photographed with the American star. This picture was taken at Nottingham and shows many of the home performers with Elder, easily identifiable by the jaunty cap which was one of his trademarks.

The news was not greeted with complete approval from the motorcycling world.

Barely had the takings from the first High Beech event been counted than the news
of the Australian invasion had the purist clubmen reaching for their pens.

A letter published in *The Motor Cycle* in March 1928 kick-started a major
correspondence about the right and wrong ways to govern and promote the new sport.
An ordinary club member with strong opinions, who in the common spirit of the times
believed one of the major aims of competitive motor sport was to provide a test bed for
technical development, wrote:

> Taken as a whole (dirt-track racing) provides good sport at present, and everyone
> admits that it thrills. It can never be the equal of our beloved road racing, which

develops machines along the lines we need. Dirt track and grass develop freaks, with stiffened frames and engines protected with wire gauze, and numerous other things quite useless for the road machine to benefit the rider in the street.

If dirt and grass track is to stay, please ACU keep it clean, stop all the freak fitments and let unaltered road machines be used. Then all will be on the same footing and we shall have real sport.

The writer was also one of the first concerned clubmen to raise the increasingly controversial aspect of the introduction of commercial promotion into the sport.

These promoters think in three letters – £ s d – smoke Havana cigars and have never enjoyed feeling a motorcycle saddle under the seat of their trousers. I ask you, are such men likely to do our sport any good?

(Left) Londoner Wal Phillips was one of the first British riders able to mount a serious challenge to the overseas stars. In 1931 he was outscoring team-mate Frank Arthur at Stamford Bridge before his season was brought to an end by injury. Phillips is also noted for being the first to ride a machine with the ultimately ubiquitous JAP engine, manufactured in Britain by the firm of J A Prestwich.

(Right) Frank Arthur, from New South Wales, ranked with Huxley and Elder as a major star of the early days of the sport, especially on his narrow and tricky home circuit of Stamford Bridge, built around the Chelsea football pitch. He later became one of Australia's leading speedway promoters.

The doubts about the effect dirt-track racing would have on the club domination of motorcycle racing were also now being voiced by those with authority and influence.

Gilbert Harvey-Kelly, president of the North West centre of the ACU, warned that the amateurish organisational skills and infrastructure possessed by the clubs – only three in England had full-time secretaries – could mean that they would loose control of dirt-track racing to the entrepreneurs.

The new sport could produce useful financial rewards for clubs, ensuring their financial well-being. He conceded however that 'the generally pitiful organisation' of the amateur sport was leaving the field open to those who were 'interested only in profit.' He wrote:

I think that dirt-track racing is going to be of great value to the sport of motorcycle racing generally, providing the ACU rules it with a rod of iron. I would beg every club in the country to use all the powers that they possess, through the ACU, to exclude outsiders trying to promote dirt track meetings.

Nip these gentry in the bud – they are only out for dividends.

Arthur Atkinson rode initially in the north for Halifax and Leeds and then turned the tables on the dominions stars by travelling to Australia, where he enjoyed considerable success. He later rode for Wembley and West Ham and after World War Two promoted with Stan Greatrex at the East London track and also with his wife Tippy at Rayleigh, Essex. He made a return to the track in the early 1950s, riding first for the *Hammers* and then for Harringay.

Sadly for the traditional clubmen, the battle for the soul of speedway was already lost. Hunting and Hoskins, having seen the commercial potential of speedway in Australia, together with the British businessmen with whom they were to quickly develop links, were not going to let slip the chance to make a profit.

The men on the high seas bound for England were not out to enjoy a holiday in the old country. They could smell the money.

High Beech did stage further club-style meetings, and there were club-organised events at Greenford in Middlesex, at Audenshaw near Manchester, at Blackpool and elsewhere. The Blackpool event, although ostensibly a club meeting, organised by the North Manchester Motorcycle Club, now managed by E O Spence from Camberley, actually raised the fears of those who opposed commercialisation.

The organisers claimed that the Blackpool circuit was the only *real* dirt-track in the country, being composed of 75 per cent sand and 25 per cent earth. The meeting at the seaside resort proved that, for the time-being at least, interest in dirt-track racing was widespread among the wider motorcycling fraternity, with a group of seasoned TT riders taking to the track.

On the darker side for the purists, *The Motor Cycle* reported on what it called 'the shadow of commercialism' that had been cast over the Blackpool meeting.

Although this event was a purely sporting one by an established club, the trade attitude began to be apparent, for at least two riders were withdrawn and the petrol and oil representatives were absent under ban from the Manufacturers' Union, or so it was noised abroad in the competitors' enclosure.

The fears of the traditionalists were certainly about to be realised. Speedway was about to take a great and irreversible leap forward, from the primitive circuit to the palatial stadium, and from the club committee room to the plush boardroom.

The appeal of motorcycle sport to a much wider public had been realised in the late 1920s, long before the huge spectator response to the dirt-track debut at High Beech. Show business entrepreneurs Fred Mockford and Cecil Smith had successfully promoted a form of mini-road racing at the Crystal Palace in South London, called 'path racing', with riders competing on circuits threading through the parkland surrounding what was generally described by the media as 'the Big Glasshouse'. Lionel Wills, a truly all-round motorcyclist himself, had been among the competitors.

Motorcycle football, using a standard ball and with goals scored in exactly the same way as in the more conventional game, was extremely popular, and drew 7,000 spectators to its own Cup Final, staged at the rugby league stadium at Headingley, Leeds.

The Brooklands Circuit in Surrey and the TT races were well established and Belle Vue Pleasure Gardens and Zoo in Manchester also staged a form of road racing. Under the guidance of E O Spence the North Manchester Motor Club held the first open British grass-track meeting to be held under the rules of the FIM – the Federation Internationale Motorcycliste – in what was later to become the famous Hyde Road speedway arena.

The arrival of A J Hunting saw rapid developments indeed. In mid-May 1928, the company he had formed with British partners, International Speedways Limited, opened up at the White City, the West London athletics arena which had been built for the 1908 London Olympic Summer Games. On the same day, in the afternoon, Mockford and Smith had staged the first speedway meeting at the Crystal Palace.

International Speedways Limited soon also began to promote at Wimbledon and Harringay, and their interests spread during 1928 to Hall Green in Birmingham, and to Manchester, to the Belle Vue Greyhound Stadium at Kirkmanshulme Lane.

Johnnie Hoskins was also now in Britain, but at this stage enjoying rather less success. He had been lured to the country mainly on the promise that there were a number of tracks ready and waiting for his promotional skills. They turned out to be more or less a figment of one individual's imagination. An exception was Hove Greyhound Stadium, on the Sussex coast, but here an excessive amount of money had been spent on track preparation, wiping out the profit. This, and complaints from residents in what was very much the genteel end of the Brighton seafront, put paid to that venture.

The capital available to International Speedways Ltd, enabling the company to promote at the finest stadia available, and A J Hunting's flair for organisation and

Australian entrepreneurs A J and Frank Hunting, who brought the first party of dominions and US stars to England in 1928, promoted through the company they formed with British backers, International Speedways Ltd, at prestigious venues such as London's White City, and the Wimbledon and Harringay greyhound stadia. When the business relationship soured, the Huntings promoted in Argentina, before returning to Australia. This picture shows Frank Hunting, third from left, with riders on board the Royal Mail ship *Asturias*, en-route to South America.

publicity, meant the brief battle for supremacy between the clubmen and the entrepreneurs was over.

The Huntings, Hoskins, Arthur Elvin at Wembley when speedway was introduced to the Empire Stadium in 1929, another multi-track operator in the person of Jimmy Baxter of Empire Speedways, and home-grown promoters like Mockford, Tom Bradbury-Pratt and Charles Knott, ensured that speedway would follow its own groove, very different to that followed by other motorcycle sports.

The entrepreneurs were careful to avoid any conflict with the Auto Cycle Union and the Royal Automobile Club, as governing bodies affiliated to the FIM. They were skilled enough to ensure that, under the umbrella of these bodies, they had sufficient control of events through representation on various internal committees and organisations, which eventually morphed into the single entity of the Speedway Control Board, to more or less run their own ship as they wished.

Dirt-track racing, now increasingly known as speedway, became a successful blend of sport – entirely professional when it came to the major tracks – and entertainment.

The sort of razzmatazz that is taken for granted in 2011, even in the once-staid sport of cricket with its 20/20 competition featuring dancing girls and blaring music when a wicket falls, was pioneered in Britain by speedway.

The new sport, having established for once and for all that the commercial promoters and not the traditional motorcycle club establishment would rule the roost, was now free to embark on its own path to the future. The road was to be a bumpy one, as the sport became noted for experiencing more than its fair share of ups and downs.

An interesting postscript to the battle between the clubmen and the entrepreneurs is provided by the attitude of Lionel Wills. The man as responsible as anyone for implanting the idea of dirt-track racing in Britain, and who had been seen as being very much in the gentlemanly tradition of the motorcycling establishment, nevertheless came down firmly on the side of commercialisation and of speedway as a sport appealing to the masses and staged in stadia with good facilities and high capacities.

He wrote in *Motor Cycling* in April 1928, when the battle between the two camps was still raging:

> Your correspondents who criticise commercialisation of the sport perhaps have not realised that someone must put up the money for a track to be built at all. Even Brooklands did not grow in the night.
>
> As long as the man with the money abides by the rules of the governing body and runs the game cleanly, I cannot see what is the objection.

Speedway at the Huracan track in Buenos Aires in 1929. The riders are, left to right, Eric Langton, Joe Gooding, and Oliver Langton. Soon after the picture was taken, Gooding crashed and broke his breastbone, collarbone and two ribs.

One of the stars at the Huracan track and a great favourite with South American fans was Yorkshireman Frank Varey, a pre-war Belle Vue star and later promoter at Sheffield and Edinburgh.

Lionel Wills continued to take a lively interest in speedway for the rest of his life. The same cannot really be said for Jack Hill-Bailey, of the Ilford club.

Described by one source as 'the gynaecologist who supervised the birth of British speedway', he continued some involvement at High Beech when the track was transformed into a pukka venue, which at one stage pre-World War Two staged league racing, but soon became disillusioned with the direction the sport had taken.

The editor of *Speedway News* at the time of Hill-Bailey's death, R M 'Sammy' Samuel, who in an earlier time had been a noted journalist in the mainstream of the motorcycling world, revealed:

> Jack Hill-Bailey's High Beech saw the days when riders came on their touring bikes from far and near. Having stripped them down they went out to race, not for starting and points money but for modest prizes.
>
> The subsequent development of speedway didn't altogether appeal to Jack's sporting instincts. The last time I spoke to him he referred to our modern tracks as 'mechanical roundabouts'.

Chapter three

ROUGHHOUSE TO RESPECTABILITY

The circus gives way to league racing

The seed planted at High Beech and elsewhere by the earliest British dirt track pioneers and their Australian and American tutors, quickly blossomed into the fully professional sporting phenomenon of speedway racing. In an age when speed was an obsession, on land, on the water and in the air, the new sport found the soil of the late 1920s and early 1930s to be fertile ground. Just as an early flowering bloom can often be cut down in its prime if the weather proves unkind, speedway soon felt the icy blasts of the economic depression and, just like a plant, survived only where its promoters had put down the most solid and enduring roots.

SPEEDWAY'S INITIAL impact, both as a club activity and as a fully-professional, stadium-based sport, had been in London and the south of England, with much of historians' focus over the years concentrating on High Beech.

As the sport spread rapidly during 1928, with the ACU granting almost 50 track licences during the year, the south of England in general and the capital city in particular generally outshone the north and midlands, both in terms of the quality of venues and the ability to attract and financially satisfy the leading Australian and American stars, and the up-and-coming home-grown racers.

The north of England was in fact the setting for one of the sport's most contrasting scenarios. It saw on the one hand the development of what was to become the most famous and long-lasting speedway club side in the world, alongside some of the most primitive and fly-by-night promotions the sport has ever known.

In London the early tracks opened by International Speedways Ltd at Harringay and Wimbledon continued to flourish, although the London White City soon fell by the wayside. These two venues, and Crystal Palace, were joined by the new track in the East End at West Ham, and in 1929 Arthur Elvin, managing director of the company running

29

Wembley Stadium, decided to add speedway to greyhound racing to provide regular income for an arena which had threatened to become a white elephant, after the end of the British Empire Exhibition for which it was originally built.

Speedway at Wembley meant a transformation in the fortunes of Johnnie Hoskins, when Lionel Wills recommended Elvin to appoint the down-on-his-luck showman to run speedway at the Empire Stadium.

Wembley's adoption of speedway also went a long way towards improving the rather roughhouse image of the sport. A J Hunting had recognised the need for a better image early on, and invited a succession of establishment-approved celebrities and even royalty to present awards at the tracks he controlled, including on one occasion King Alfonso of Spain.

In the north and in Scotland, speedway seemed a less smooth and professional operation than further south, despite temporarily using a venue as prestigious as the Celtic Football Club stadium at Parkhead.

The one shining exception to the general rule of southern speedway dominance, during virtually the whole of the sport's first 40 years in Britain, was Manchester's legendary Belle Vue. After the early activity in the north west at Droylsden and later at Audenshaw, three stadium venues in Greater Manchester presented early speedway.

International Speedways Ltd and the Huntings promoted in 1928 at the Belle Vue Greyhound Stadium at Kirkmanshulme Lane, in the Gorton area of East Manchester. They faced opposition from another company operating at the Manchester White City Stadium in the Old Trafford area of the city, close to the famous football and cricket grounds, and from the Albion Stadium at Salford, in which the pre-Wembley Johnnie Hoskins had an interest, as he sought a permanent post in British speedway.

The Kirkmanshulme Lane venue was not an overnight success, and there were fears that the Huntings would not renew their interest in 1929. The two other promotions also had their ups and downs. Fortunately for the city and for speedway as a whole, Manchester possessed two trump cards, each with a belief in the future of speedway racing.

Eric Spence, formerly of the Camberley Motorcycle Club, was a much admired figure within the world of the motorcycling establishment. Unlike many of his fellow club figures, he also possessed a true entrepreneurial spirit, to add to his knowledge of the motorcycle world and his administrative abilities.

Spence's confidence that speedway had a role to play in the north west was shared by another equally visionary personality and, crucially, one with a solid business position and access to significant financial resources. John Henry Iles was the managing director of Belle Vue (Manchester) Ltd, the company formed in 1925

Today's speedway stars wear lightweight Kevlar racing suits and safety equipment includes state-of-the-art back protectors. At the start of the 1930s riders like Joe Gooding were relying on two-piece leathers and a body belt around the waist to provide some protection. Although Gooding may well have only been posing for a publicity shot, the pullover, collar and tie tells of a more formal if less well-protected era in speedway as in everyday life.

Sheffield Speedway Team 1931

to buy out the interest of the Jennison family, who had run Belle Vue since its inception in the 1840s.

An amusement park operator, who had developed the iconic Dreamland complex at Margate, Iles saw the potential for making speedway an integral part of the overall experience at the pleasure gardens.

He was generally interested in sport, and had begun to develop a fairly basic sports facility within the Belle Vue complex (completely separate from the greyhound track down the road at Kirkmanshulme Lane), into what he intended to become a major venue. Iles' vision saw professional football and top class rugby league as the mainstays of the stadium.

One of Manchester's two famous football clubs, City, had moved from East Manchester to a new venue elsewhere and Iles sought to fill the gap in Gorton by launching a new club, Manchester Central. The aim (never realised) was that the club would eventually join City and United in the Football League.

Speedway, on a track built around the pitch designed for both codes of football, would be a natural addition to the sporting line-up. Evening racing would attract a fair proportion of the people who had spent the day enjoying the venue's other attractions, and those who did not have to travel long distances after the speedway could also be tempted back into the fairground, ballrooms and bars, to spend even more money.

To run the speedway, and give it an air of motorcycling respectability lacking at other venues, Iles turned to E O Spence and the North Manchester Motorcycle Club. He acquired a majority stake in the club, and appointed Spence, who combined the

Sheffield competed in the northern section of league racing in 1929, 1930 and, as pictured here, in 1931. Second from left in this team group is a young Tommy Allott, who was still riding in the early 1950s. Allott's brother Guy founded a speedway dynasty, with his son Nicky and grandson Adam also taking up the sport. The other riders are, l-r Eric Blain, Norman Hartley, Gus Platts, Bronco Dixon, George Corney, and Dusty Haigh.

When Arthur (later Sir Arthur) Elvin introduced speedway to Wembley in 1929 he appointed Johnnie Hoskins as speedway manager, on the recommendation of Lionel Wills. Johnnie's son Ian became the Wembley mascot and is pictured on his Fruin special machine, accompanied by his father on an AJS, about to take a spin around the Empire Stadium.

Wembley's opening for speedway was not popular with Hoskins' great rival A J Hunting, who refused initially to allow any of his contracted riders to appear at the Empire Stadium. The response from Hoskins was to raid other clubs, particularly in the north of England, for talent. One of the riders he recruited was George Greenwood (below), who started his career with Leeds.

attributes of a born entrepreneur and administrator with an established reputation as a long-standing official in the motorcycling world, to run the speedway.

Iles had the money, Spence had the reputation and the know-how. For many years to come, the front cover of Belle Vue's programmes proclaimed that meetings were run under the auspices of the North Manchester Motor Club'. It was the perfect combination for speedway success, especially in an era where the mushrooming spread of the sport produced, particularly in the north of England, a rash of often unsuitable and primitive venues and fly-by-night promoters.

Britain in the late 1920s was fertile ground for the development of a professional sport like speedway racing. In London and the south east, where production of the new consumer goods was concentrated in modern factory units, in the midland cities where the growing motor trade had become established and was prospering, and to a lesser degree in the cities of the north, where the Wall Street Crash and the ensuring world depression had still, in 1928, to occur, there was cash for the working class to spend and reduced working hours to allow them to enjoy life.

Speed itself was an obsession, with the heyday of the Brooklands circuit for both two and four-wheeled motor sport, the exploits on both land and water of Sir Malcolm Campbell and his succession of ever-faster Bluebird vehicles, and the quickening pace of development in the air, celebrated by the Schneider Cup races, which led indirectly to the development of the Spitfire fighter plane.

Personal transport, whether it be the motorcycle, often with a sidecar for the wife and children, or the increasingly mass-produced family motor cars of the day, was seen not as a gas-guzzling threat to the environment, but a great liberating factor for the masses.

For the wealthy, including pioneer speedway rider and populariser Lionel Wills, the mode of road transport was not a small Ford or Morris but a Rolls-Royce. Nevertheless, Lionel's contemporary view, quoted some years later by his son Peter, that the internal combustion engine was 'the apotheosis of civilisation' would have been widely shared. It was hardly surprising speedway should find such a receptive audience nationwide.

Some of the tracks which managed to gain ACU approval to stage the sport in 1928 were so anxious to jump on to the bandwagon that they defied deteriorating weather conditions, opening their doors well into the late autumn.

Manchester and its neighbouring city of Salford initially had three major speedway tracks, in addition to the other circuits within the Lancashire conurbation at Droylsden and Audenshaw. This is the Manchester White City team of 1930, when the circuit had been taken over by the Belle Vue management from its previous promoters. Pictured l-r are Max Grosskreutz, Wilf McClure (manager), Frank Charles ,Wally Hull, Fred Strecker and Cyril Wilcock. The man in the hat (right) is Belle Vue speedway chief E O Spence.

Vic Huxley made the transition effortlessly from the individual racing of speedway's early days to team racing. Huxley also continued to shine in individual events, winning the *Star* newspaper sponsored British Championship in 1930 (he also finished runner-up on no less than three occasions, was British Match Race Champion in '31 and '34 and London Riders Champion in 1936.

The geographic spread more or less covered the nation, from Bristol in the south west to Middlesbrough in the north east. The midlands saw activity in Birmingham, Coventry, Leicester and Wolverhampton, tracks opened across the industrial heartlands of Lancashire and Yorkshire, and along the south coast at Brighton, Portsmouth, and Eastbourne.

In Scotland there were meetings at Glasgow's White City Stadium and Carntyne dog track as well as at Celtic Park, and in Edinburgh, while in Ireland racing was staged in both the Free State and Ulster, in Dublin and Belfast respectively. The United Kingdom picture was completed by the opening of a track in Cardiff as late as Boxing Day 1928.

Curiously, given the fact that East Anglia was to become, and remains to this day, a speedway hotbed, the first activity (on grass) at The Firs in Norwich had to wait until 1930, with the first cinders being spread on the track a year later.

This rapid expansion inevitably embraced a wide variety of venues, with an even wider variation in the standards of the racing surfaces employed, the safety features, pits and dressing room accommodation for the riders, and spectator facilities.

The rough and ready end of the speedway venue spectrum can be divided into two specific groups. The first were the venues where the promoters, either individuals, consortia or motorcycle clubs, were well intentioned but handicapped by lack of capital for long-term investment.

The second group were the speculators who saw a quick profit in the new craze, to be achieved for a minimal financial outlay. The attitude that all that was required in 1928 was to find a suitable playing field, spread a few cinders on a marked-out grass track, and perhaps erect a rickety grandstand, and then stand back and take money at the turnstiles, did exist.

In 1929 Nottingham's Olympic Speedway, initially developed by the local Tornado Motorcycle Club, was fairly rudimentary, but at least had a properly constructed track and a boarded safety fence. When the Nottingham team arrived at Cardiff they were shocked by what was later described as 'a thin strip of dirt sprinkled on the outside of a rugby football field.'

The first speedway to be seen in the West Yorkshire town of Halifax was not at the later football ground venue of The Shay, but at the Thrum Hall cricket ground, where

Nottingham had a fairly undistinguished time in the top tier of British speedway, finishing bottom of the National League in 1930 with just two wins from 24 matches. In 1931 the club withdrew mid-season because of injuries and falling crowds. The team in the early part of the season, pictured after riding a match, judging from their grimy faces, is l-r (standing) Ernest Houlton (team manager), Bert Fairweather, Nobby Kendrick, Billy Ellmore, Joe Gooding, and Fred Strecker. Kneeling are George Wigfield and Reg Lucas.

the track was reportedly almost circular and where the first meeting was illuminated by acetylene flares.

Staying in Yorkshire, Barnsley's Lundwood Stadium was described as having been built on a hillside, with no stands or other spectator amenities and only rudimentary pit facilities for the riders. The safety fence was composed of a continuous mound of turf, built to a height of around three feet.

At the other end of the spectrum to the grab the quick profit and run brigade were the men who had the vision to see that, properly organised, speedway had a long-term future.

The existence of the greyhound stadia– the sport had been introduced to Britain at Belle Vue in 1927 – offered speedway ready-made venues of a high standard. The downside was that the ready availability of these stadia meant that, for the most part, speedway singularly failed to develop its own purpose-built arenas.

The leading greyhound stadia in the late 1920s had facilities that the majority of professional football grounds were unable to match. The football grounds had been developed piecemeal and, intended primarily for an all-male, working class audience, possessed little in the way of civilised amenities or creature comforts.

In contrast, the purpose-built greyhound stadia, and those arenas adapted for the purpose, were designed for all-year round use. From the earliest days, they featured plenty of seating, covered accommodation, bars and even restaurants, to attract both male and female punters.

The various methods of starting races tried in speedway's early days – including push starts and rolling starts – all proved unsatisfactory and on occasions crowds became enraged by stewards continually re-starting heats or excluding riders for anticipation. Fred Mockford, promoter of Crystal Palace (and later New Cross) and rider Harry Shepherd, pioneered the starting gate, which owed much to horse racing. Mockford, in plus fours, is seen trying out his invention. Control of the gate later passed to the steward or referee, who operated it electronically – still the case today.

Speedway's decision to move in to the greyhound arenas – a quite understandable move at the time – proved in one sense to be the absolute making of the sport. In another sense, it was a move whose consequences were to haunt speedway forever.

The owners of greyhound stadia, both in London and in the provinces, only rarely promoted speedway themselves on their own premises. Exceptions to this general rule

The Firs at Norwich, later to develop into one of speedway's best-supported centres in the provinces, originated as a grass-track speedway.

were Wembley, and Harringay, where in later years the cinder sport was run by the powerful Greyhound Racing Association (GRA).

Speedway promoters were tenants, paying rent for the use of the stadium facilities, including office space and sometimes mechanical workshops for maintaining the bikes. The speedway men were responsible for constructing and maintaining the actual track and for erecting a safety fence, a starting gate, and the coloured light signals used for racing. In most instances the greyhound arenas had track lighting that could be adapted for use for speedway.

Before any activity took place on the speedway track, whether practice or an actual meeting, the greyhound track had to be completely covered in some form of protective sheeting. Given the delicacy of a greyhound's feet, and the speed at which the dogs race, a collision with a lump of cinder or shale thrown up from the adjacent circuit could prove damaging or even fatal to the animal.

The expense and trouble of putting down and taking up the sheeting, liberally covered with loose cinders or shale, can be imagined. In almost all instances too, the income from the sales of drinks, meals and other refreshments was retained by the stadium owners.

Speedway had its ready-made venues, but the problems its managements faced with the greyhound promoters became legendary. Ian Hoskins, who promoted in the immediate postwar era at Glasgow White City, recalled in later years how the owners 'for years played snakes and ladders with the rent they charged the speedway promotion, always in the up direction'.

A fairly flimsy barrier on top of a modest grass bank is all that separates the crowd from the track at 1930s Norwich.

A classic action shot of Vic Huxley from the 1930s.

The policy of too many greyhound stadia owners was to extract as much rent as they could from speedway promoters without raising the stakes to the point where the speedway management simply pulled out.

The essential shape of speedway moved forward significantly in 1929. Throughout 1928, meetings were usually composed of individual events for a variety of golden or silver helmets, gauntlets and sashes. Racecards consisted of heats and finals for these awards, handicap races, and match races between two leading riders.

Promoters relied on the reputations of the early stars to pull the crowds in through the turnstiles and in most instances, the response was gratifying and financially rewarding.

In that first season, speedway essentially resembled a travelling circus of experienced Australian, New Zealand, and American stars, gradually joined by emerging English favourites, who toured the country accompanied by frenzied publicity.

Billy Lamont, the Australian nicknamed Cyclone, was dubbed 'The Man with a Month to Live' because of his fence-scraping style of riding. Eventually, as Lamont survived to appear at the tracks across Britain, even the dimmest of fans realised that it was proving to be a long month.

The more far-sighted promoters, who were in the sport for the long haul rather than for a quick profit, sensed that more was needed if speedway was to survive as a major attraction. The first tentative steps towards team racing were taken in the latter part of the first season, proving popular with the fans who were looking for something a little more substantial than the simple spectacle of broadsiding.

In a shot taken from the spectator's viewpoint at Southampton in the 1930s Vic Huxley attempts to drive inside fellow Australian Steve Langton.

Team racing was in fact to prove the essential step forward. For 1929 two leagues were formed, the Southern League, composed of the London tracks and other teams from south of the River Trent and the English League, which had 18 original entrants, 17 from north of that cultural divide and Leicester Super, the Midland's city second venue, which had an Australian-style track length, at 586 yards, and staged races over three rather than four laps.

As so often in the sport's history, it was to be the southern-based competition which thrived. The record books prove that the southern dominance of speedway during so much of the sport's existence is not some sort of imagined cultural discrimination.

During the lifetime of the original National League, from its formation in 1932 to its final season in 1964 – roughly the period covered by this book – Belle Vue (on five occasions), Swindon (in 1957), Southampton (in 1962) and Oxford in the last year, were the only clubs outside of London to win the championship of the top division. In the capital, Wembley won titles on eight occasions and Wimbledon on seven.

In that same period of time there were a further 26 league titles to be claimed, in either the original 1930s Provincial League, Divisions Two and Three of the National League (including the 1946 Northern League and the 1952/53 Southern League), and the 1960s reincarnation of the Provincial League; the Southern Area League not included.

Only four of those titles went to teams in the north of England; Middlesbrough won the Northern League (the second tier competition that year) in 1946 and the National

League Division Two the following year. Hanley (Stoke) were Division Three champions in 1949, and Newcastle won the 1963 Provincial League title.

The remaining championships not won by London teams went to tracks in the south, the midlands, the west country or East Anglia.

The 1963 season, which saw success at the top level for Belle Vue in addition to the Newcastle victory, was an echo of the uncompleted final pre-World War Two season in which, ironically, Belle Vue and Newcastle led their respective sections at the time racing was suspended.

It was, perhaps, an omen of things to come that the 1929 debut of league racing saw such a difference in fortunes between the Southern and the English (Northern) organisation.

The Southern League, starting with eleven teams, finished with ten, Birmingham Hall Green resigning mid-campaign. The finishers all completed their 20 league fixtures, and Stamford Bridge took the championship by two points from their closest challengers, Southampton.

In the north, it was a much more complicated, and much less successful, business. One of the original 18 entrants, Long Eaton, did not race a single league fixture, probably because initial open meetings at the Derbyshire track were relatively poorly supported.

In addition five tracks resigned during the course of the season. White City, Manchester, quitting following a dispute that arose *after* they had won the championship. The title was handed to Leeds. Of the others to resign, Manchester Belle Vue apparently withdrew in disgust at the standard of organisation within the league,

The Harringay National League team of 1936. L-r, Fred Strecker, Les Wotton, Norman Parker, Jack Parker, George Kay (manager), Jack Ormston, Bill Pitcher, Dicky Smythe, and Billy Dallison. Kneeling is Bob Lovell.

while Burnley, Bolton and Hanley probably pulled out because of poor support.

The eleven clubs that constituted the final league table rode varying numbers of matches, from the 24 achieved by Preston and Rochdale to the mere 18 staged by Newcastle.

For 1930 the Southern League expanded to fourteen starters, including the previous year's drop-out club, Hall Green. History repeated itself to the extent that the second Birmingham side, Perry Barr, followed the 1929 lead of their neighbours and resigned in mid season. The other starters, including the luckless Nottingham, who won just two of their 24 league fixtures, made it to the finish line, with Wembley winning the championship, again ahead of eternal bridesmaids South-ampton.

After Wembley, the magnificent Custom House arena at West Ham was speedway's finest stadium, with a two-tier stand designed by sports ground architect Archibald Leitch that would today be listed, and a nominal capacity of 100,000 spectators.

A degree of chaos continued to reign in the north of England. Belle Vue, having got over their spat on administrative practices, beat neighbours White City to the title. The league, including for the first time Scottish teams from Edinburgh and Glasgow, had 13 finishers, but there was a huge variation in the number of fixtures completed.

Belle Vue ran up a total of 39 points, winning nineteen of their 21 matches, drawing one and losing one. White City won 13 of their 15 matches, but would still have been narrowly beaten (by two points) even if they had achieved fixture parity and won the six additional matches. At the other end of the scale Newcastle (Gosforth) raced just nine matches.

In 1931, the final year of regional leagues, Wembley repeated their 1930 Southern League triumph. To show that confusion was not entirely confined to the north of England, Nottingham resigned midway but their results to that point were retained in the final league table, Coventry replaced Leicester mid-stream, and a Belle Vue II side ensured that the Manchester club had a foot in both camps by replacing Harringay in mid-season.

Speedway's ups and down throughout the 1930s, after the initial goldrush period had subsided, can be seen to rise and fall in parallel with the economic barometer of the nation. The north, in speedway as well as economic terms, lost out.

The first National League, in 1932, ran for half the season with ten teams, six of which were in London, two in the north (Belle Vue and Sheffield), one in the Midlands

(Coventry) and one in the West Country at Plymouth. Stamford Bridge won this initial championship but the second half of the season featured a separate competition, the National League Championship, run without Sheffield, and won by Wembley.

Essentially, after the collapse of all but two northern sides at the end of the 1931 campaign, league speedway until the middle of the decade consisted of a central core of between five and seven clubs in London and a changing cast of provincial sides, consisting of Southampton, Coventry, Leicester, Nottingham, Sheffield, Plymouth, and Birmingham (Hall Green).

Team racing undoubtedly proved to be the saviour of speedway after the initial circus period. Today, with the obvious exception of the Grand Prix series, successor to the long-running World Championship competition which will be considered in detail in the following chapter, individual events are not as popular as the league and cup matches between the clubs.

The major advance for speedway in the 1930s, apart from the establishment of a settled, if at times relatively small league structure, was the growth in demand for an international element to the sport, both in terms of team and individual racing, an aspect covered in detail in chapter six.

Chapter four

STABILITY AND SURVIVAL

Speedway's strangest era

The mid-1930s represented speedway's strangest era. The sport had contracted drastically from its initial boom in the late 1920s and the early part of the decade. Yet although the closure notices had been posted from one end of the United Kingdom to the other, the sport nevertheless thrived and retained a high profile in London and Manchester, launched a prestigious World Championship competition and maintained well-supported test matches against Australia. It even managed to expand from 1936 onwards, until the outbreak of World War Two abruptly switched the focus from growth to mere survival.

S PEEDWAY, WHICH in the late 1920s and early 1930s had spread its tentacles into virtually every part of Great Britain, was by the middle of the decade in headlong retreat back to its original strongholds of London and Manchester.

League racing had initially penetrated as far to the south west as Plymouth, north east to Newcastle and across Hadrian's Wall to Glasgow.

As the global recession sparked by the Wall Street Crash of 1929 started to bite, money for entertainment became non-existent in the industrial centres of the north-east, Lancashire and Yorkshire, and was much tighter even in the less hard-hit cities of the midlands. Speedway as a nationwide activity became, for a while at least, a victim of the recession.

For the 1934 season, after Coventry, Nottingham and Sheffield had withdrawn from the National League, the competition was restricted to the hotbeds of the capital city, to Manchester, England's second city of Birmingham and, surprisingly, Plymouth, as ever out on a limb in the south west peninsula. The message seemed to be that, when times were hard, a huge population was invariably necessary to ensure crowds were sufficient to make the sport profitable.

The naval city of Plymouth was to prove an exception for the time being, although keeping the sport alive in the south west was a struggle.

For 1935, even the populace of Birmingham proved insufficient to keep speedway running at Hall Green. Speedway was now back to its absolute heartlands.

It was a situation that had some parallels with the boom to bust to revival story that was to follow in the 1950s. In that later era, the major difference, as we will eventually see, was that the London centres, rock solid in the 1930s, were also victims of a slump in the sport's popularity.

Speedway's own recession in the mid-1930s came as a shock not only to fans across the country who had grown accustomed to spending an evening at their local track, but also to a large group of riders who found themselves struggling to stay involved.

During the mushroom growth in the late 1920s and in the early years of the 1930s, when nearly 30 league tracks and a variety of open-licence centres operated at the peak of the boom, riders had flocked to take advantage of the opportunities to be paid for taking part in an activity they loved.

Comparatively few were able to demand and receive the huge sums reputed to have been earned by the major performers of the day, particularly Lloyd 'Sprouts' Elder, Vic Huxley and other superstars of the era.

Now, with the competition for really competitive rides getting hotter and hotter, many of the sport's journeymen riders found themselves increasingly pushed to the margins.

For the 1934 season the promoters attempted to make some provision for the huge pool of by now under-employed speed men by establishing a second division, effectively a reserve league. All the tracks, with the exception of Lea Bridge (replaced by Walthamstow in mid-campaign) and Plymouth took part.

Riders were graded and only those in the B category were permitted to compete in the second tier, in four-a-side teams racing matches over six heats. Given the highly restricted opportunities at the top level, many well-known names were reduced to what, in reality, ranked little higher than the more customary second half scratch races.

In 1933 Belle Vue had begun a spell of absolute domination of British speedway. That year saw the first of four successive title wins and five on-the-trot successes in the National Trophy, coupled with four victories in the ACU cup. A triple crown for the

The midway point of the 1930s, with league tracks reduced to just seven, six in London and Manchester's Belle Vue, was a low point for speedway. The sport was further plunged into gloom when a rider who might have gone on to set unassailable records had he lived was killed in 1935 at the age of just 24. Tom Farndon, born in Coventry, was involved in a track crash with team-mate Ron Johnson at their New Cross base.

Manchester side in four separate seasons was true domination. No blasé London fan could complain of poor competition from the country cousins when Belle Vue visited metropolis.

The only other team to get its hands on national silverware in the period 1933 – 1936 inclusive was West Ham, whose reserves pipped Wembley to the second tier title when the competition was staged in 1934.

Throughout the period the frustrated London tracks had to be content with success in their own highly prestigious team-based competition, the London Cup. In the four seasons between 1933 and 1936 it was well shared out, with wins for Wembley, New Cross (in the

Speedway's retreat into the metropolitan areas of London and Manchester was reversed in 1936 with the formation of a second division, known as the Provincial League. Although over the two seasons 1936-37 the new competition never had more than a maximum of seven tracks, and lost teams in mid-campaign, it was a fair success. Southampton recorded a Provincial League and Provincial Trophy double and are seen celebrating with promoter Charlie Knott on the far right of the group.

track's first season after transferring from Crystal Palace), Harringay and Hackney Wick.

The safety valve of the reserve league was absent in 1935. The National League tracks, Harringay, West Ham, Wembley, league newcomers Hackney Wick, New Cross and Wimbledon, to place them in their finishing order behind Belle Vue, represented league speedway in Britain.

It was the lowest point ever in the history of league racing in this country. When the National League, nearing the end of its useful life, was reduced to seven clubs in 1963, its junior partner the Provincial League was thriving , with twice as many operating tracks.

The much-travelled Les Wotton's career stretched from 1928, when he rode in the first-ever meeting held in his native Bristol, to 1951, when he retired after Southampton withdrew from the sport in mid-season. He rode in all three Divisions of the National League, was an England test performer, toured Australia and was a *Star* championship finalist on three occasions.

League speedway overall was not at risk in 1963 and the sport was on the cusp of another era of prosperity.

Strangely enough, despite the shrunken league, there was no serious chance of the game going out of business in 1935 either.

This fact alone contributes to the view that the mid-1930s was without a doubt the most curious period in the entire history of British speedway.

Shrunken to a rump of seven competitive tracks, the sport was in other ways absolutely thriving. Belle Vue and most of the London circuits were enjoying good crowd levels, and the fans seemed content with seeing the same faces performing week after week.

London, as usual, had escaped the worst effects of the recession, while Belle Vue, as always, was a case apart, with speedway benefitting not just from its own hard-core fans but from the thousands who poured into the Manchester zoo and pleasure gardens, perhaps as their only summer break, and attended the speedway as a finale to the day's entertainment.

Speedway in the second half of the 1930s, buoyed by the creation of a second tier, was starting to take on an appearance that would still be familiar to fans in the 1950s. This photograph taken by a fan, Dick Smart, at Nottingham in 1937 shows that more riders have adopted a foot forward approach, rather than the leg trailing technique, while cornering.

It was a little like a cosy, self-contained club, with everybody happy except the unfortunate unwanted riders who had entered the sport during the boom years and now found themselves on the outside looking in at the National League's private party.

Speedway was not, of course, all about league racing. Throughout the 1930s individual contests, including match races, continued to draw the crowds. *The individual aspect of the sport, closely allied to the growth in international competition, is covered in detail in the following chapter.*

In 1935, the closest challengers to Belle Vue's league supremacy proved to be Harringay. The North London team were beneficiaries of the closure of Birmingham Hall Green, which had been run by the same promoter, Tom Bradbury-Pratt.

Jack and Norman Parker formed the spearhead of the Harringay side, with Jack Ormston, Bill Pitcher and Les Wootton joining from Birmingham, and keeping riders of the calibre of Billy Dallison, Dicky Wise and Alec Statham in the lower reaches of the line-up.

The run of success enjoyed by Belle Vue, and repeated in later decades by the likes of Wembley and Wimbledon, was made possible by relatively stable team composition. Today, a championship win in speedway is often the prelude to a team losing riders, to ensure a measure of team strength equalisation.

Belle Vue in 1935 were theoretically weakened by the temporary retirement of Frank Varey and the transfer to Wembley of Frank Charles. As the results show, the strength in depth represented by the likes of Eric and Oliver Langton, Bill Kitchen, Max Gross-kreutz, Joe Abbot, Bob Harrison and a supporting cast kept the Hyde Road side comfortably on top of the table.

Fashions changed considerably through the 1930s, with the West Ham riders wearing racing suits not unlike those that have come into vogue in the 21st century (minus the sponsorship and advertising stickers of course, in the inter-war era). Pictured are, back row, l-r, Tommy Croombes, Eric Chitty, Bronco Dixon, Charlie Spinks, Tiger Stevenson, Johnnie Hoskins (promoter), Ken Brett, Bluey Wilkinson, Rol Stobbart. Front. Arthur Atkinson, George Saunders, Ian Hoskins (mascot) and Mick Murphy.

The 1936 season was one of those tipping points that occur in the history of any sport, and particularly in speedway.

After the period of contraction, the sport turned outwards again from its established fortresses and began to rebuild its bases in the provinces, at the same time providing real racing again for riders who had begun to despair at the lack of chances to truly compete.

The establishment of the Provincial League in 1936 was a relatively low-key affair, unlike a similar event nearly a quarter of a century later. Nevertheless, the importance of the new competition to the riders cannot be overstated.

Cardiff, Plymouth and Southampton had all run successful open licence meetings in 1935, and they were joined in the Provincial League by Bristol, Liverpool and Nottingham (the latter side being promoted by the same management as Cardiff).

Each track was required to lodge a deposit of 100 guineas as a guarantee and the men behind the competition believed a 3,000 gate would constitute a paying proposition.

Each team was allowed to sign nine riders, who would receive a weekly payment of 50 shillings (£2 50p) maintenance money. The riders were to be guaranteed one home and one away meeting a week. There was to be no start money but points money would be paid at the rate of 10 shillings (50p) a point.

By contrast to West Ham, the Nottingham riders of 1937 pose in a way that was still familiar many years later for team shots. Five of the seven riders raced for some years after World War Two. L-r, Frank Hodgson, Fred Tuck (putting two fingers up to the photographer!), Fred Strecker, Tommy Allott, Sam Marsland, Ted Bravery. George Dykes, the captain, is on the machine.

There was also to be a supplementary National Provincial Trophy competition, and Johnnie Hoskins entered a West Ham reserve side, named the *Hawks*, with many of the team's 'home' matches being staged at Southampton. This competition would pay 10 shillings a start and 10 shillings a point and the organisers of the Provincial League estimated that a top rider could earn, in theory at least, £25 a week.

In the late 1960s, when speedway was enjoying another period of prosperity, the author was taken on a tour of Nottingham White City Stadium by Fred Strecker, one of the riders to benefit substantially from the new Provincial League. Strecker had been one of the pioneers, switching from grass-track racing to dirt-track at the end of the 1920s, and during his career he was associated with Manchester White City, Belle Vue, Nottingham (his home-town), Harringay, Hackney Wick, Leeds, Stoke and Norwich.

What the smartly-dressed men about speedway were wearing in the late 1930s. Pictured at Hackney are the Wick's management duo of Fred Whitehead (left) and Fred Evans, with New Cross and former Crystal Palace promoter Fred Mockford on the right.

Nottingham and Leeds (where the Fullerton Park Greyhound Stadium venue lay in the shadow of Leeds United's Elland Road ground) are the strongest contenders for the title of the most prominent pre-World War Two venues not to stage speedway after the end of hostilities.

The Nottingham stadium was well-appointed, with seating and plenty of covered terracing, resembling Owlerton at Sheffield in both its layout and the length of the track (380) yards. After the war, the greyhound racing operators set their faces rigidly against speedway, and the venue closed for the inevitable redevelopment, in this case as an industrial estate, in 1970. During our tour of the White City Fred Strecker recalled:

> The Provincial League really was a godsend. Once the teams outside London and Manchester started to close down, to league racing at least, there were an estimated 150 riders, many with considerable experience in the National League, who could only get a ride in second halves, or on the open licence tracks.

for **STRENGTH & STAMINA**

FAMOUS SPEEDWAY RIDER

LIONEL VAN PRAAG

relies on **SEAGERS EGG FLIP**

The Bracer that Builds you up!

"My job demands absolute physical fitness at all times, so I rely upon Seagers Egg Flip for the strength and stamina that is essential in speedway racing. I have found it to be of the greatest value in keeping me up to the mark."

56 PER FULL-SIZE BOTTLE

L. Van Praag.

THE HOUSE OF SEAGER ESTABLISHED 1805. DISTILLERS OF FINE GIN FOR OVER 130 YEARS

No overt sponsorship in the late 1930s but top riders routinely endorsed various products in advertisements in the speedway and general press. Alcohol endorsement would be frowned upon today but Lionel Van Praag is happy to confirm that it is central to his stamina training.

When you had been used to riding with a contract and being guaranteed a certain number of meetings and rides, it was very hard to be more or less pushed out of speedway.

With a regular league spot, how much you could earn obviously depended upon how well you did out on the track, but at least the chances were there for you to try and take. During the 1934 and 1935 seasons you rarely knew where you were going to get a ride next and a lot of people just packed their equipment away and more or less called it a day.

The Provincial League was a qualified success, although many of the arguments that were already familiar in the sport and were to be repeated on many occasions in many different eras were present.

Fred Strecker linked with Southampton for the initial Provincial League season and, like other riders from the south coast side, also appeared during the campaign for promoter Charles Knott's other interest, National League Harringay.

Southampton won both the championship and the supplementary National Trophy ahead of Bristol, with the two major competitions providing each team with a total of 26 matches.

A blow to the league was the closure of Cardiff in June 1936. The previous year's open-licence meetings had been well supported, but the crowds surprisingly did not turn out for the supposedly more attractive league fare. The demise of Cardiff had a positive effect upon sister track Nottingham, where gates had slumped to around 2,000, not enough to support even racing designed to be far more economical to stage than in the National League.

Although the Cardiff company continued to promote at Nottingham for a while after the Welsh track had closed, the saviour of the White City was Hackney Wick chief Fred Whitehead. Nottingham had already been strengthened by the return of George Greenwood, who had previously ridden for the midlands side in the National League and another Wembley man, Cliff Parkinson was also added to the line-up.

Although the Provincial League riders had been promised two meetings a week as a minimum, there was a period soon after the Cardiff closure when the competition seemed to grind almost to a halt, with only three matches being completed in the space of a fortnight.

A question mark seemed to hang over the future of the entire competition. The salvation of the league as a whole has been attributed to the tour of its tracks made by Putt Mossman's All-American team, which included riders of the quality of future World Champion Jack Milne and his brother Cordy.

Large crowds were attracted wherever the Americans competed and the Provincial League had the impetus to complete the season.

George Greenwood became the first name to be inscribed on the Provincial League Riders Championship Trophy, clinching the title in the final round of the competition on his home track at Nottingham. Contemporary reports spoke of a considerable amount of team riding in the event, with fellow Nottingham riders continually attempting (with much success) to block out Greenwood's main challenges.

Speedway News gave only a half-hearted welcome to the Provincial League when it reviewed the competition's first season. It admitted that Greenwood, who had suffered injury and loss of form resulting in him being excluded from the Wembley National League side, deserved a break, but added:

> We welcomed the Provincial League as a recruiting ground for new talent and thought it would be a good idea to include a few experienced riders to set a standard the newcomers must reach as soon as possible. But winning matches seems to have become an end in itself. The Provincial League Championship was instituted to give young riders a chance to compete under championship conditions. Again the original idea has been completely lost sight of and the first eight riders in the final placings have all ridden for at least six years.

The magazine appeared to have lost sight of the fact that paying spectators were in the mid-1930s (and remain to this day) unwilling to see the worthy but often hardly thrilling efforts of raw novices. Established names, then as now, attracted the crowds and the Provincial League provided opportunities for the dispossessed riders and re-distributed an alarmingly localised sport over a much wide part of the country.

The National League continued on its way in 1936 with little change, Belle Vue again taking all the major honours.

Change came in 1937, when the Manchester side slipped to a mid-table position. Two major losses affected Belle Vue, with a broken leg for Bob Harrison causing him to miss two months of the season. The loss of Max Grosskreutz was more permanent, with the Australian star at Provincial League newcomers Norwich.

The National League title went for the first time to West Ham, who finished the season four points ahead of Wembley and New Cross.

In the 1937 Provincial League, Southampton, Nottingham, Bristol and Liverpool re-surfaced for a second season. In addition to Norwich, they were joined by other newcomers in the shape of Leicester and Birmingham. The season proved to be a mixed one, with Leicester withdrawing after just six matches, to be followed later by Liverpool, which was promoted by Belle Vue's E O Spence.

Spence in fact transferred the Liverpool fixtures to Belle Vue, ensuring that the Provincial League finished the season with six teams. Bristol were champions, swopping places from 1936 with Southampton. Nottingham, after many years of almost constant failure, won the sup-

In 1938 E O Spence was still very much in charge at Belle Vue. This souvenir of the Aces was issued with one of Manchester's evening newspapers and shows, clockwise from number one, Bill Kitchen, Bob Harrison, Ernie Price, Oliver Langton, Walter Hull, Eric Langton, Frank Varey, Jack Hargreaves and Oliver Hart with Spence, as ever, at the centre of things.

BELLE VUE SPEEDWAY TEAM, 1938.

1. W. KITCHEN.   2. BOB HARRISON.
3. OLIVER HART.   4. E. PRICE.
5. JACK HARGREAVES.   6. OLIVER LANGTON.
       7. MR. E. O. SPENCE (Direction and Clerk of the Course).
8. FRANK VAREY.   9. ERIC K. LANGTON, Captain.   10. WALTER HULL.

plementary Provincial Trophy, ahead of Bristol, and there was a second success for the east midlands side when they beat Southampton 98-69 on aggregate to lift the Coronation Cup.

Speedway's increasing stability brought a successful year in 1938, the last season to be fully completed in the pre-war period.

There was another new name on the National League Championship Trophy, that of New Cross, who finished ahead of previous year's champions West Ham and Wembley. In a rare instance of promotion/relegation, the 1937 Provincial League champions Bristol had swapped places with Hackney Wick, who despite finishing just third from bottom of the National League that year had struggled financially.

The re-named National League Division Two was a much more substantial competition, with nine starters and nine finishers. Not, admittedly, exactly the same starters and finishers. The financial difficulties Fred Whitehead experienced at Hackney had not been helped by the fact that, despite the team's double trophy success, Nottingham had lost money in 1937. A new promoter took over at the White City for

Even as blatant a showman as Johnnie Hoskins would probably have hesitated before putting his own name on the front cover of a programme. Former rider Arthur 'Westy' Westwood was a flamboyant character who in 1938 controlled Nottingham, Leeds and Birmingham Hall Green in addition to Sheffield. At the end of the season, the Speedway Control Board deprived Westwood of all four track licences.

1938, Arthur Westwood, but he stayed only long enough to make sure the team completed its fixtures in the curtain-raising English Speedway Trophy, which at least meant he retained his pre-season deposit paid to the league.

Westwood, who was also promoting in Division Two at Sheffield and Birmingham Hall Green, transferred the Nottingham fixtures to Leeds, where he had intended to run open licence meetings only. The Nottingham fans had complained bitterly when Westwood had distributed key members of their strong 1937 side among his other tracks.

Hackney's step down to Division Two was rewarded when they won the initial championship, on race points only, from Norwich.

In other competitions, Wimbledon won the National Trophy (Division One final) by beating Wembley and Norwich, just pipped on the post in the league, secured a first title by beating Hackney Wick in the Division Two final. West Ham beat Wimbledon in the ACU Cup but the Dons also celebrated a London Cup final success against New Cross.

Speedway's new-found stability carried across into the 1939 season, although the preparations for war being carried out across the country, with plans for gas masks and the evacuation of children marred the spring and summer months.

There were again seven teams in Division One, with 1938 wooden spoonists Bristol changing places with Southampton. Racing was suspended at the end of August, just before war was actually declared on September 3 1939, with Belle Vue holding a single point lead over Wimbledon, and with third-placed Wembley just a further point behind.

Division Two had started the season with eight teams but during the course of the campaign a revived Crystal Palace and Middlesbrough withdraw and Stoke's fixtures were taken over by Belle Vue Reserves, with the Manchester promotion again stepping into the breach to ensure the second tier competition remained viable.

Another revived venue, Newcastle, topped the Division Two table at the time racing was suspended, six points ahead of Hackney Wick. The table was effectively meaningless, as Newcastle had ridden 15 league matches at the time, while third-placed Sheffield had only completed eight.

Early season competitions had been completed before the suspension of racing. Belle Vue (British Speedway Cup), Wimbledon (London Cup), Newcastle (English Speedway Trophy North) and Norwich (English Speedway Trophy South) getting on to the list of the final pre-war silverware holders. Sheffield won the National Trophy Division Two final, beating Hackney Wick, but the Division One final of that competition, between Belle Vue and Wembley, was never contested.

Speedway had settled down to a period of stability by 1939 but there was still a rapidly revolving door for some riders. This shot of Norwich, promoted by Australian test star, Australian Champion and former Belle Vue rider Max Grosskreutz (centre of the picture in the roll-neck sweater), shows former Nottingham men George Dykes (left) and Fred Strecker on the machines. After Nottingham closed in 1938 they rode for Leeds, Stoke and, finally, the Norfolk side.

One final competition, the Union Cup, was notable for re-introducing competitive speedway to Scotland. Both Edinburgh (Marine Gardens) and Glasgow White City took part in the northern section of the competition. The winners of the north and south sections were due to meet in a final, but the Union Cup was also a casualty of the outbreak of war.

British speedway was approaching the end of its twelfth season when World War Two intervened. It had been a roller-coaster ride, from the boom that followed the High Beech experiment, through the start of league racing, the virtual extinction of the sport in the north, and later in the midlands and elsewhere, as the recession bit hard, followed by the revival prompted by the Provincial League and the relatively healthy state of affairs in 1939.

The state of emergency in the late summer of 1939 followed by the actual start of hostilities not unnaturally prompted the authorities to crack down on all forms of entertainment. As the war got into its stride, it became apparent that sport was good for morale, and gradually many activities, particularly professional football, resumed a reasonably full programme, essentially of regional competitions to avoid excessive travel.

Although so much of speedway racing, at the highest level, was centred in London, there never seems to have been any serious consideration of staging even a limited league programme, or indeed regular speedway of any kind in the wartime capital.

The war years did in fact see some speedway in London. There was a single meeting at the Crystal Palace in 1940, organised by the ENSA organisation for the entertainment of servicemen, open licence meetings at Harringay between 1940 and 1942, and meetings at West Ham in 1940, 1941 and 1942.

New Cross was quick to stage speedway after the end of hostilities, with five meetings starting in June 1945. Wimbledon was badly bombed, with the grandstand and offices destroyed, and damage was still apparent in some areas of the stadium when the sport resumed in 1946.

Outside the capital, Glasgow staged six open licence meetings in 1940, and Oxford operated in 1940 and again in 1941. The original Rye House training track, operated by former Australian international Dicky Case, staged racing between 1940 and 1943 inclusive.

Birmingham's Alexander Stadium at Perry Barr, where speedway had been staged in 1928 and which after the conflict was to be the home of the *Brummies* from 1946 to 1960, at one stage held Italian prisoners of war.

The slight but redoubtable figure of Miss Alice Hart helped keep the sport alive at Belle Vue during the war years and through the immediate post-war era. In this post-war shot she is surrounded by staff and riders including Jack Parker (leaning out of cab), George Smith, Ken Sharples, Ron Mason, Jack Chignell and Bob Harrison (far right).

The London tracks which dominated speedway in the 1930s advertised heavily in *Speedway News*, helping to keep the publication viable. World Champion Lionel Van Praag is the major attraction at Harringay when Wembley are the visitors.

In the provinces Sheffield, Norwich and newcomers Bradford Odsal also staged meetings after victory had been declared in 1945.

Despite these acknowledged meetings in wartime – perhaps 60 or so while the conflict was still raging – it was left to the north and Belle Vue, to really keep the sport alive in the years 1940-45 inclusive. What happened during those war years at Hyde Road has become the stuff of legend.*

The bare statistics show that Belle Vue staged weekly racing within the season from September 23 1939 to October 20 1945, when most other speedway venues were closed and shuttered. Some 170 individual meetings were run, plus some novice events.

Miss Alice Hart, who took over as manager at Hyde Road when E O Spence assumed wider responsibilities at Belle Vue, had as her aim the entertainment of the public and the maintenance of their morale, while also having the vision to look ahead to a post-war future.

Belle Vue had traditionally kept racing fuel on hand at Hyde Road and this proved the foundation of the wartime supply. Machines were made available for visiting riders. No petrol was available for the tractor to grade the racing surface, and all meetings were held during daylight hours.

Most of the riders who took part in wartime meetings either lived within easy reach of Manchester, or were members of military units stationed locally. Riders from farther afield who found they were able to make it to a meeting were usually accommodated, with some regular performers willing to stand aside.

As the tide of the war turned and victory approached, Miss Hart concentrated more and more on providing opportunities for younger riders through the Belle Vue training school.

More than 30 riders participated in wartime meetings at Hyde Road, including many service personnel. The most highly-decorated of these was the Danish rider Morian Hansen, who had taken part in the first-ever World Championship Final in 1936. Hansen, who rode in the UK for West Ham *Hammers*, Hackney Wick and Bristol *Bulldogs* in the 1930s, became a pilot and was awarded the Distinguished Flying Cross, among many other awards.

Happily, the majority of the Belle Vue wartime riders survived the conflict to return to the sport when league racing resumed in 1946.

One who did not was the Canadian George Pepper. With Newcastle in pre-war days he, like Hansen, became a pilot and he too was awarded the Distinguished Flying Cross. Sadly, Pepper was killed when his aircraft was involved in a training accident becoming perhaps the most high profile speedway casualty of the conflict.

---

* The Belle Vue wartime story is well told in the book *Speedway in Manchester 1927-45,* by Trevor James and Barry Stephenson.

Chapter five

TOWARDS A WORLD-WIDE SPORT

Speedway goes global

The creation of league racing in 1929 was a natural development once promoters realised that there was a limit to the appeal of competition for seemingly endless gold and silver cups, helmets, and gauntlets. Test matches, given the number and strength of the Australian riders active in the sport in Britain, were a further natural progression. Although overseas riders from outside the British Commonwealth and the United States were comparatively rare throughout the sport's first decade, the huge global potential was recognised with the arrival in 1936 of a World Championship event.

THE DEMAND for an international element to speedway racing at British tracks came in the first season, with representative matches between home and overseas riders, the latter drawn exclusively from the dominions and America.

Organised international competition, in terms of both individual championships and matches between the home riders and their overseas counterparts soon followed.

Given speedway's propensity for wrapping what is quite a simple activity in a complex web of regulations and scoring systems, baffling to the casual spectator, the major individual events in the inter-war years were often complex, while international team clashes too have over the years attracted considerable controversy.

Although league and international matches have formed the sport's bread and butter, the jam has been provided by the elite individual tournaments, of which the supreme example, for some 60 years, was the World Championship.

The competition has its origins as far back as 1929, with the *Star* Championship, sponsored by the London evening newspaper of that name. In its first year the *Star* Championship was contested between riders selected from those competing in the Southern League. To complicate matters from the outset, there were in fact two separate competitions, one for the experienced riders from Australia and America – thought to be far superior to their home- grown counterparts – and one for the emerging British stars.

The contest was run on a match race basis, with two riders in each of the heats, the semi-finals and the final. Roger Frogley won the British section, defeating Jack Parker (so often the bridesmaid rather than the bride in big individual events), while Frank Arthur defeated Vic Huxley in an all-Australian overseas final.

In 1930 all of the 12 riders selected for the championship took part in a one-off final at Wembley with Huxley the winner, but in 1931 there was an eliminating round at each Southern League track, with 20 qualifiers competing in a Wembley final won by the American Ray Tauser.

The 1932 *Star* National Championship embraced northern riders for the first time and Belle Vue's Eric Langton took advantage by beating Australia's Vic Huxley in the final. The following year's final was won by Tom Farndon of Crystal Palace, Jack Parker made up for his earlier disappointment by triumphing in 1934, while Frank Charles was the last winner of the championship in 1935.

This final was overshadowed by the injuries sustained the evening before, in South London, by Farndon, now riding for New Cross, and his team-mate Ron Johnson. Farndon was to die of his injuries a few days later.

Although the *Star* Championships had embraced a variety of different formats, the first ever official World Championship, which culminated in a final at Wembley on September 10 1936, was an even more complicated affair.

The final at Wembley was preceded by a qualifying competition. In later years, riders who qualified for the one-off final, no matter how they had performed in the qualifying events, started the big night on equal terms.

In 1936, and again in 1937 and 1938 (the 1939 Final did not take place because of the outbreak of World War Two) riders were awarded bonus points during the qualifying events, which they carried forward to Wembley.

On the night, the Australian Bluey Wilkinson won all of his five heats. But he had accumulated fewer bonus points on the road to Wembley than the men who on the night proved to be his chief rivals.

When the scheduled heats had been completed, Wilkinson's ten bonus points and his 15 points scored on the night gave him a total of 25. It was only sufficient to give him third place in the World Championship.

Fellow Australian Lionel Van Praag, who had recorded 12 bonus points en route to the Final, was the second highest scorer on the night, with 14, taking his total up to 26. Third place man during the evening's racing proved to be England's Eric Langton. He had 13 points to his credit on the night, one less than Van Praag and two fewer than Wilkinson, but the 13 he had amassed during the qualifying events brought him level with Van Praag and ahead of Bluey.

The first-ever World title was thus to be decided by a run-off between Van Praag and Langton. When the riders lined up, Langton broke the tapes. With Van Praag reportedly claiming that he did not wish to win the World title by default, Langton was not excluded.

The two riders set off again, with Langton leading until the final bend of the last lap, when Van Praag edged through a gap left by the Englishman.

Langton could never have been nicknamed 'Smiler' at the best of times, and generally appeared to glower at the camera. His particularly sour expression on the winners rostrum appears to have been due not to any fundamental disagreement with the complicated bonus points system as much as his belief that Van Praag had reneged on an alleged pre-run-off agreement.

This was subsequently claimed to have comprised a deal that whoever arrived at the first bend in front would go on to win, with the prize money being split. Speculation has continued ever since as to whether Van Praag was simply unable to resist the small gap that Langton left for the Australian to pass him on the final bend, or considered that his sportsmanship in agreeing to a re-run after his opponent had broken the tapes at the first time of trying released him from the deal.

This method of deciding the World Championship, although controversial, was repeated for the 1937 championship, when the American Jack Milne scored maximum points on the night enough, with his bonus points, to give him a clear three point margin over runner-up Wilbur Lamoreaux, and a five points lead over his brother Cordy in third place.

The system remained in place too in 1938 for what was to prove to be the last pre-war final. This time however, in the view of many fans, justice was done. On the night Bluey

Top left: The aftermath of the inaugural World Championship in 1936. A pleased but perhaps slightly sheepish Lionel Van Praag receives the trophy, while runner-up Eric Langton of England characteristically glowers at the camera. Van Praag defeated Langton in a two-man run-off to decide the destination of the title, at the end of a controversial Final. (The John Chapman Archive)

Top right: Australian Bluey Wilkinson was unbeaten on the night at the 1936 World Final but because the scoring system in use at the time also took into account bonus points gained in qualifying events, he was relegated to third spot behind Van Praag and Langton. Happily Wilkinson was the undisputed and highly popular winner of the World crown in 1938 and is seen here with the trophy.

The 1937 World Champion was American Jack Milne. In contrast to Van Praag's endorsement of the alcoholic Seagers Egg Flip, Milne attributed his success to Ovaltine.

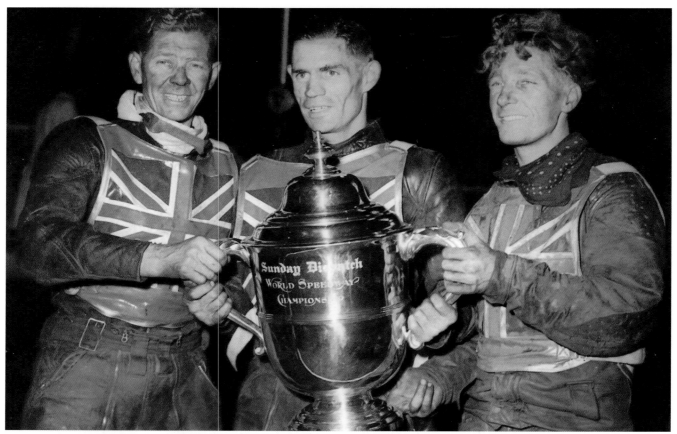

The first post-World War Two final was not held until 1949 and saw a never-to-be-repeated 1-2-3 success for England. Tommy Price of Wembley was champion with Belle Vue riders Jack Parker (left) runner-up and Louis Lawson third.

Jack Biggs of Australia was hot favourite to win the 1951 World Final at Wembley after victories in his first four rides. But in his final heat Biggs was crowded out and had to settle for third place behind fellow Aussie Jack Young of Edinburgh, the only Division Two rider to win the World title, and Split Waterman of England.

TOWARDS A WORLD-WIDE SPORT

(Left) Peter Craven became only the second Englishman to win the World title with victory in 1955 (Freddie Williams of Wembley, winner in 1950 and 1953 was a proud Welshman). Craven won again in 1962, a year before his track death, and on that occasion is pictured with runner-up Barry Briggs (right) and third-placed Ove Fundin of Sweden. Briggs (four times) and Fundin (on five occasions) were to have their own World Final triumphs.

(Right) The late 1960s saw the end of the Briggs/Fundin era in the World Championship and the start of the amazing run of success of six-times champion Ivan Mauger of New Zealand.

Wilkinson tied on points with Jack Milne, having held off Milne's brother in the penultimate heat to take a clinching second place. The fact that Wilkinson had one more bonus point than Jack Milne gave him an acclaimed title.

Although the initial 1936 final had featured riders from just four nations – England, Australia, the USA, and Denmark – the qualifying rounds had encompassed representatives from seven other nations, including France, Spain and Germany.

In 1937 Danish star Morian Hansen was the sole competitor from the European continent and his absence in 1938 meant that England, Australia, the United States and Canada monopolised the event. The 1939 final was a casualty of the outbreak of war.

Test match action from Wembley in 1932. L-r Dicky Smythe and Vic Huxley of Australia (in dark jerseys) head Ginger Lees and Jack Parker of England.

The horses for courses policy of England and Great Britain test selectors, who routinely selected plenty of home-track riders for matches, is evident at Belle Vue in this 1930s picture. Jack Parker (far left), later to become an *Aces* star, leads a line up reading l-r Tommy Croombs, Eric Langton (BV), Tom Farndon, Joe Abbott (BV), Bill Kitchen (BV), Tiger Stevenson and Bob Harrison (BV).

The first three seasons after World War Two saw much of the world, especially the mainland of Europe, in turmoil, and travel difficulties and other factors ruled out an immediate return to a World Championship event.

The first post-war World Final was at Wembley in 1949 and produced the first and only instance of the English riders on the winners' podium. Wembley's Tommy Price became the first English victor, with Jack Parker second and Belle Vue discovery Louis Lawson third.

Wembley was to remain as the undisputed home of speedway's big night until 1960. Although crowds slimmed down somewhat from the 93,000 who witnessed the English triumph in 1949, the final remained a big attraction, drawing coachloads of fans from all over the UK in addition to contingents from overseas.

Even after speedway's mid-1950s slump, with so many track closures, it remained the custom for the surviving supporters clubs of dormant teams to arrange an annual outing to Wembley.

The traditional race jackets depicting a kangaroo for Australia and a lion for England were retained until the 1950s, when they changed to emblems depicting the flags of the respective countries. This Australian line-up consisted of, back row, l-r, Arthur Payne, Keith Gurtner, Arthur Simcock (manager), Jack Young and Aub Lawson. Front row, l-r, Johnnie Chamberlain, Ronnie Moore, Peter Moore and Jack Biggs.

When Ronnie Moore decided to become a New Zealander for speedway test purposes, Australia became Australasia. Here Moore leads from Australian Peter Moore and English riders Arthur Wright and Eric Williams.

The first England-Sweden test series was staged in 1956. Ove Fundin of Sweden leads the field on his home-track at Norwich. Sweden won the series 2-1 but despite Fundin's best efforts, England sole success came in the match pictured.

(Left) The colours of Canada were carried in the 1937 World Final by Eric Chitty of West Ham, pictured with his daughter.
(Right) Swede Rune Sormander joined Leicester in the late 1950s.

The British Isles had a second winner in 1950, when Welshman Freddie Williams took the crown – like Price he was a Wembley rider – and the competition recorded its biggest surprise to date in 1951, when Australian Jack Young, at the time riding in Division Two of the National League for Edinburgh, triumphed (securing, at the same, time, a transfer for a record fee to Division One West Ham).

Young won again in 1952 and Freddie Williams recorded his second victory a year later.

Howdy Byford of West Ham, third from left, a former Japanese POW, led this group of English riders who competed in the Olympic Stadium in Amsterdam in 1948.

There then followed an astonishing period of 14 seasons when the World Championship was shared between just five riders – the 'Big Five', whose dominance in British domestic racing in the National League meant that for a period of time they were handicapped, starting yards behind their opponents.

The domination by the five riders of the World Championship saw wins in 1954 and 1959 for Tasmanian-born Ronnie Moore, who later adopted New Zealand nationality for speedway purposes, in 1955 and 1962 for Peter Craven of England, in 1957, 1958, 1964 and 1966 for Barry Briggs of New Zealand and in 1965 for Bjorn Knutson of Sweden.

These records were surpassed by the final member of the 'Big Five', Sweden's Ove Fundin, who won in 1956, 1960, 1961 (when the final was held away from Wembley for the first time, in Malmo, Sweden), 1963 and 1967. The sequence was broken in 1968, a turning point for speedway, when New Zealander Ivan Mauger, won the first of three titles in a row and six in total.

John Carpenter, later of Leicester, gained much of his earliest experience racing in Holland. He is the rider holding the giant bouquet in this 1948 picture.

Mauger had first arrived in England in 1957, as a 17-year-old, and struggled to win a place at Wimbledon, the track where Ronnie Moore and Barry Briggs were established stars. With Craven and Fundin also established stars in the 1950s (Knutson emerged somewhat later), the rise to super stardom of the superbly stylish, Mauger, immaculately organised mechanically in both workshop and pits, in the late 1960s was yet another indication that speedway was passing from one era to the next.

After World War Two, both the replacement British Riders Championships of 46,47 and 48, and the first post-war world final in 1949, gave the honour to the man who won on the night.

The one-off final format, which survived until the end of 1994, seeing finals staged in Sweden, Poland, the United States, Germany, Holland, and Denmark, in addition to Britain, produced some intriguing results over the years, with the result influenced by many factors, including machine troubles, a niggling injury sustained in an early ride but not sufficient to prevent a rider continuing his

One of the earliest Swedish riders to race in league speedway in Britain was Olle Nygren.

There was team racing as well as individual events in Holland in 1948 and John Carpenter is pictured in the colours of the Dutch Lions.

The Swedish team
competed in an early
World Team Cup
competition. The picture
was taken at the Prater
Stadium in Vienna, and
shows, l-r, Gote Nordin,
Bjorn Knutsson, Ove
Fundin (on the bike), Per
Olaf Soderman, team
manager Arne Bergstrom
and Rune Sormander. The
girl is unknown but the
man in the trilby hat is
Richard Kudelka, who
assisted the Swedish
riders in Austria as a
interpreter.

The Swedish team competed in an early World Team Cup competition. The picture was taken at the Prater Stadium in Vienna, and shows, l-r, Gote Nordin, Bjorn Knutsson, Ove Fundin (on the bike), Per Olaf Soderman, team manager Arne Bergstrom and Rune Sormander. The girl is unknown but the man in the trilby hat is Richard Kudelka, who assisted the Swedish riders in Austria as a interpreter.

challenge, and just simple nerves at a crucial stage. The vagaries of fortune gave the occasion a unique frisson.

Today's Grand Prix series, which replaced the one-off finals in 1995, may be reckoned by many to be a fairer indication of all-round ability over a gruelling series of events. As such, it is perhaps closer in spirit to the original bonus points system.

International team speedway in 1930 inevitably meant England versus Australia. Given that the only other meaningful sporting exchange between the Lions and the Kangaroos at that time was in cricket, it was perhaps inevitable that the matches should be labelled as tests.

Official England v Australia tests began in 1930, when the Lions beat the Kangaroos 4-1, despite Australia having won the very first match, at Wimbledon, by 35 points to 17. There had been unofficial meetings ever since 1928, and these were to continue in parallel to the real thing for many years, both in the UK and down under.

The first official Australia v England series raced down under took place in the Australian summer of 1934-35. The British Auto Cycle Union maintained that this was the only pre-war English tour that they deemed to be official, although the speedway authorities themselves gave their blessing to events in 1935-36, 36-37, 37-38 and 38-39.

The parallels between the speedway matches and the cricket series extended only as far as the countries involved and the series title. Although English cricketers in tests down under have had to acclimatise to unaccustomed heat and to the fanaticism of crowds often more than twice the size of those grounds in England were able to accommodate, matches in both countries have generally been played on what could be described as a level playing field.

While Australia over the years have admittedly won many more cricket test matches overall than England, that has almost always been purely a matter of the respective playing strengths of the contestants. In speedway, England versus Australia tests, both in the UK and down under, have always been governed by a complex system of checks

and balances unknown in cricket. Some of the factors favoured the Australians, some the English.

Australian speedway tracks are invariably much bigger than English circuits. The majority of the Australian riders contesting the tests not only had experience on some, or most, of their test tracks, but also rode for league teams in England, at test venues.

The only other venue in England used for a World Championship Final was the giant Odsal Stadium, Bradford, which staged the event on three occasions after Wembley became unavailable for speedway.

One of several incarnations of the World Championship Trophy, won by Peter Craven in Belle Vue, to add to the Golden Helmet Match Race Championship Trophy.

Speedway was one of the first sports to be flexible about nationality. Here New Zealander Ivan Mauger represents Great Britain in an international at Wembley.

All too often, many of the English test riders were confronted with unknown Australian tracks on which they could be completely at sea. In England the Australian riders were for the most part attached to Division One circuits, and were familiar with all of the test venues.

Despite the usual vagaries of selection, it has also been normal for cricket elevens to be comprised of the best players available in either country. It could scarcely be argued that some of the England test teams sent to Australia consisted of the seven or eight leading riders qualified to appear for the Lions.

Particularly in post-war years, England teams selected to go to Australia often depended upon who was available to travel or indeed was willing to go away for so long. The Australian riders earned a major part of their living in England and were present any way during the English season.

When an England party set off on the boat journey to Australia, their only hope of augmenting the strength of the selected test party was to enlist English-qualified riders wintering down under either attached to individual tracks and promotions or touring with other, unofficial, England teams.

In England, the success or otherwise of an Australian test team depended to a large degree on how many Aussie riders were available during any one season.

The English selectors often adopted a horses for courses policy, naming home riders for a one-off test in a series, which did not always fully succeed.

In both England and Australia, the actual make-up of the team was governed not only by the selectors believing home track riders would be more successful, but also taking into account their supposed ability to increase crowd numbers.

(Left) England's first World Champion Tommy Price prepares for his first ride at Wembley in 1949, unfazed by the number thirteen race jacket.

(Right) Test match action from Wimbledon as England's Arthur Wright attempts to go around the outside of Peter Moore of Australia. Moore was a notably fast starter but was susceptible to pressure from a pursuing rider.

In general terms, the home side has usually dominated speedway tests, with England for the most part having been able to track much stronger and more representative teams in the inter-war years than after World War Two, a fact reflected in the results.

England won nine out of ten series raced at home pre-war, being successful in 31 matches to Australia's 15. In Australia, the home side won all five of the pre-war series, with a similar success ratio when it came to individual matches, the Kangaroos winning 17 tests to 8.

The post-war years, up to the effective end of almost continuous official tests in 1953, saw England triumph on four occasions to Australia's three, the Lions winning 15 matches to the Kangaroos' 16.

Interest was waning in the England-Australia tests. Although a great many test and international series or one-off matches have taken place on British tracks since 1953, involving England v Australasia, versus Sweden, Poland and other nations, the genre had undoubtedly lost much of its magic by the time reduced crowds and the difficulty of raising a strong Australian team called an end to the original series begun in the UK in 1930.

Perhaps the truest mark of speedway's global success in the twenty-first century is the fact that the Grand Prix system encompasses meetings in countries as varied as the Czech Republic, Italy and Croatia, in addition to Great Britain (the Millennium Stadium in Cardiff), Poland, Sweden and Denmark.

One unexpected effect of the sport's globalisation has been two-fold. Riders in the British top tier league competition, the Elite League, today often ride for clubs in Poland and Sweden, where league racing flourishes, as well as for their British teams.

In addition, it is not uncommon for a British Elite League club to field a seven-man team without a single British-born rider.

Chapter six

INTRODUCING A GOLDEN AGE

Post-war prosperity overcomes all obstacles

After the gloom and virtual close-down of World War Two, speedway bounced back in 1946 to achieve a level of success and a geographical spread, both in Great Britain and across the globe, that would have been unthinkable in the 1930s. Yet during the sport's most glorious period it had to endure official disapproval, punitive taxation and a range of practical problems that would have deterred a bunch of men and women less determined than speedway promoters.

BRITAIN IN 1946 was bombed-out, tired-out, shabby and virtually bankrupt. The 'Great' in the country's title, despite the wartime courage of the nation's citizens and their prime role in defeating the dictators, was hanging on by a thread.

For six long years the country and the people had endured the darkness of the blackout, the tyranny of the ration book, and the uncertainties and anxieties of total war. The national debt had piled up, leaving the government in financial thrall to the world's new super-power, the United States of America.

The return of speedway racing on a regular basis nationwide restored the colour to what had become grey Britannia. The sport's revival was the perfect antidote to the overall feeling of austerity.

Once a week, initially in major manufacturing and commercial centres like London, Glasgow, Manchester, Birmingham, Sheffield, Newcastle, Bradford, Norwich and Middlesbrough, and subsequently across wide swathes of England, and in Scotland, and in Wales, league speedway provided one evening at least of colour and excitement for the workers and their families.

Given the enormous boost to morale provided by the return to regular racing, it would have been perfectly logical to have expected the powers-that-be in the land to give speedway every encouragement.

Sadly, the very opposite proved to be the case.

Clement Attlee, who headed the post-war Labour government, claimed to be a sports fan. He demanded that the county cricket scores were made available to him as regularly as the minutes of Downing Street cabinet meetings. His Tory rivals also considered themselves, in their own terms, to be sportsmen, with many spending the parliamentary vacation on the grouse moors of Scotland and the Pennines.

Cricket, rugby union, huntin', shootin' and fishin' were the preferred sporting pastimes of the great and the good. They realised too, as vote-seeking politicians, that too much interference with professional football and rugby league, the traditional sporting outlets for the working man, was a potentially a perilous venture.

Speedway racing, almost totally discounted by authority pre-war, hardly seemed to matter. Until, that is, the first post-war season of 1946 saw the dirt-track game attract an unprecedented crowd level of six and a half million people, arousing wild enthusiasm.

The government, desperate to boost not only industrial productivity and exports to restore the nation's war-shattered economy, but also its own authority, saw midweek evening sport as an encouragement to absenteeism in the factories and workshops of the major industrial cities and regions.

Ministers and senior civil servants initially demanded a complete ban, safe in the knowledge that the main activities to suffer – speedway and greyhound racing – would be the ones they believed would not involve much if anything of a political backlash.

Dog tracks saw their meetings cut at one point to just one a week, but after an outcry and a campaign by more enlightened MPs, highlighting the positive role speedway played in actually encouraging greater productivity, speedway was reprieved.

Ministers and senior civil servants accepted the right of the sport to operate on its traditional race nights – but at a shocking price. The price was the imposition of entertainment tax on speedway at 48 per cent (later to rise for a short while to 52 per cent) – a figure far, far in excess of the 15 per cent levied on professional football.

There is absolutely nothing to suggest that Attlee, the mild-mannered, pipe-smoking, public school-educated socialist, whose place in British political history is assured as the creator of the National Health Service, ever learned to care about the results of the Harringay *Racers* or the New Cross *Rangers* as he unquestionably did about the performances of Middlesex and Surrey County Cricket Clubs.

Nevertheless, three years on from the planned assault on speedway's midweek matches, with the need to gain re-election looming, something unprecedented did occur. With annual attendances now topping the 10 million mark, and with the sport attracting mainly working class audiences in areas where Labour was the predominant political force, Attlee acknowledged speedway's popularity and vote-attracting potential.

When the World Championship was resumed in 1949, the Prime Minister dispatched his wife to present the awards at the Wembley final. The political spin doctors of the day, had they existed, would have rubbed their hands with glee at the icing on the cake of that night's triumph (never to be repeated) of English riders finishing in the top three positions.

In 1950, with speedway still riding high in the popularity stakes, Attlee's government was re-elected, albeit with a narrow majority. This proved to be serviceable for just a year, and with speedway itself starting to worry about its shrinking crowds, the electorate then said goodbye to the man who tried to ban the sport.

The immediate post-war era in speedway has been well documented, both in a substantial number of individual club histories, rich in statistics, and in the author's own overall narrative account of the era, *The Golden Age of Speedway* (The History Press 2011).

After Belle Vue's wartime heroics, and the short seasons of meetings staged at some tracks in 1945, a real return to something like normality came in the spring of 1946.

Perhaps normality is a poor choice of word, for what actually occurred was decidedly out of the ordinary. Two leagues were formed, each with six participating teams, comprising the National League as the top tier and the Northern League as its junior partner.

The London giants of Wembley, West Ham, New Cross and Wimbledon, with Belle Vue and the only immediate post-war newcomer, based at the massive Odsal Stadium in Bradford, formed the National League.

The Northern League embraced Middlesbrough, Sheffield, and Newcastle, stretched the credibility of its title a little by including Birmingham and Norwich, and was completed by the welcome return of league racing to Scotland after a long absence, represented by Glasgow White City.

A year after the 1946 comeback season, speedway virtually doubled in size, adding three teams to what now became the National League Divisions One and Two, and creating a new Division Three, with eight tracks.

From this point onwards, speedway's story was one of almost unbroken extension, until the number of starters for the 1951 season reached an unprecedented 37 league tracks.

When league racing returned in 1946 the majority of the riders involved had raced prior to the war. Here Tommy Price of Wembley goes inside Cliff Watson of West Ham in a National League clash.

Over the same period of time as the expansion of league racing, the sport had re-established test matches against Australia, re-instated the World Championship (in 1949, after three years of a substitute British Riders Championship) and supported the individual Match Race Championship, pitting the holder against a nominated challenger in a two-man contest that at its peak was a huge crowd attraction.

Jack Parker, now with Belle Vue, so often the bridesmaid rather than the bride on big occasions, had his day when he lifted the British Riders Championship trophy in 1947.

The 1948 season belonged to Harringay's Australian star Vic Duggan, who was virtually unbeatable and was reported to have earned the then huge sum of £5,000 for the season.

The vast crowds being attracted to the sport, and the general air of optimism, to a substantial degree masked the reality of the fact that, easily detectable now with hindsight, but not so obvious to the majority on the ground, that speedway had actually peaked, not with the record number of tracks in 1951, but a couple of years earlier, in 1949.

That was the year when aggregate crowds reached their highest level, of somewhere in the region of 11 million people, an impressive figure but one which was never to be reached again.

After the high point of the late 1940s and very early 1950s, speedway suffered a relative decline. The professional three division structure became just two leagues for 1954, and after the withdrawal from racing in 1957 of the iconic Wembley *Lions*, following on the early death of the sport's great champion at the Empire Stadium, Sir Arthur Elvin, the remaining eleven clubs merged into a single competition, backed by four Sunday afternoon training tracks, semi-professional at best, in the guise of the Southern Area League.

Birmingham, drawing huge crowds to the Alexander Sports Stadium at Perry Barr, were promoted to Division One for 1949. American Wilbur Lamoreaux, runner-up in the 1937 World Final, moved to the Brummies from Wembley to add weight to their first top tier campaign.

Although the World Championship, still being staged as it had been from its inception at Wembley, continued to be a major draw, and an event that gave the sport a good deal of its media credibility, one-time major elements of the fixture list such as the test series against Australia declined as both contests and crowd-pulling attractions.

Wilbur Lamoreaux's daughter Jeanette pronounced her favourite *Brummies* rider to be Geoff Bennett, a rider who first raced on Army tracks in Italy just after World War Two and became a star in the then-new Division Three at Cradley Heath in 1947. Jeanette is pictured with her father (right) and Bennett before a meeting.

That is taking the story ahead just a little too quickly. Returning to the revival of the sport in the first few intoxicating seasons after the return of peace, it appears amazing to the modern eye that speedway's administrators, the Board of Control which consisted of nominees from the motor sports' governing bodies of the Auto Cycle Union (ACU) and the Royal Automobile Club (RAC), together with the individual track owners and managers, were able to satisfy so quickly the enormous hunger for speedway that quickly became apparent nationwide.

In that first season of 1946, with just 12 league tracks operating, the provision of sufficient riders was just about achievable. An initial grading into different categories and subsequent distribution on a basis of theoretical equality to the teams, achieved reasonably balanced sides.

Belle Vue's wartime meetings had been contested by some 36 riders, either on a regular or occasional basis and although not all emerged to ride in the first season of

Speedway in Scotland enjoyed a golden era in the early 1950s. At Glasgow Ashfield Johnnie and Ian 'MacHoskins' dance a Highland Fling on the centre green with their riders.

revived league racing – Frank Varey opting to retire from racing and promote at Sheffield – most of these helped to form the core manpower for speedway in 1946.

They were joined by those whose wartime service had kept them largely overseas or, if in the UK, well away from Manchester.

Leicester's Blackbird Road re-opened for Division Three speedway in 1949 and the local *Hunters* were promoted to Division Two in 1951. A packed grandstand sees action against Walthamstow, London's only second tier track.

Division Three produced exciting, if at times less sophisticated racing than the higher divisions. Here Long Eaton take on eventual champions Poole in 1951.

Men who had worked in essential war industries, often because they were considered too old for front-line military service, became available once again.

The 1946 teams inevitably had a high average age, with the majority having at least some pre-war speedway experience. Although the Belle Vue meetings had placed more emphasis on encouraging new talent once it was clear the war was coming to a successful conclusion, only a limited amount of the newcomers were available for the first year of peacetime league racing.

The amazingly rapid expansion for 1947 required both additional venues and a great many additional riders. Where did the venues and the manpower come from?

The early 1950s saw the not particularly successful debut of future World Champion Peter Craven, who rode briefly for his hometown team of Liverpool before moving to eventual glory with Belle Vue.

Finding the tracks presented enough of a problem. Although the vast majority of the significant number of venues which had staged speedway at some time in the 1920s and 1930s were still in existence, many were either now closed to speedway for one reason or another – Stamford Bridge, Crystal Palace, Nottingham and Leeds were examples – or needed considerable expenditure to make them suitable for revival, at a period when such building materials as were available were largely reserved for the purpose of building new homes for returning servicemen, or patching up war-damaged factories, ports, and steel plants.

Odsal, Bradford, the home since 1934 of Bradford Northern Rugby League Club, was a vast but largely undeveloped amphitheatre, created from a former quarry, and capable of attracting (at a time when health and safety provisions were much looser) a hundred thousand or more spectators to its rough, largely un-terraced cinder banking.

Johnnie Hoskins, who had served as a civilian instructor in the RAF during the war, re-opened both Newcastle and Glasgow White City (subsequently to be run by his son Ian) for short seasons in 1945. Hoskins was nevertheless beaten to the punch on the acquisition of the speedway rights at West Ham Stadium, where he had reigned supreme in the 1930s. He joined forces with local interests to promote at Odsal, giving Belle Vue the club's first-ever really serious north of England rival.

Bradford was the only brand new track out of the twelve operating in 1946, and even in 1947, with the opening of eleven additional circuits, only four, Wigan in Lancashire, Cradley Heath in the Black Country of the West Midlands, Tamworth in Staffordshire and Wombwell in South Yorkshire, were absolute newcomers.

Speedway riders were major celebrities in the post-war golden age. Not everyone liked it, including Leicester man John Carpenter and particularly his wife Leah, who was suspicious of the female fans who constantly pursued the riders. Here John and Leah receive a gift from Leicester assistant manager Ted Flanaghan to mark their wedding.

Over the years from 1947 to the mid-1950s, despite the difficulties of obtaining even such simple materials as wiring and timber for safety fences, let alone much more substantial bricks and mortar for new spectator facilities, speedway did find new homes, widely spaced across the country.

By no means all of these were the traditional greyhound stadia utilised in the 1930s. Football grounds of different degrees of seniority and with a wide variation in spectator facilities were developed for speedway at Halifax Town's The Shay (not the pre-war venue at the Thrum Hall cricket and rugby league grounds), at Hastings, Edinburgh Old Meadowbank, Glasgow Ashfield, and Fleetwood.

Speedway has always promoted itself as a family sport where the fans are concerned and there have been many instances of brothers, fathers and sons competing with and against each other over the years. Here Jack Parker (left) of Belle Vue and brother Norman, of Wimbledon, enjoy a conversation.

This time it's a Welsh threesome. Twice World Champion Freddie Williams (left) and his brother and Wembley team-mate Eric (right) have secured a booking at the Empire Stadium for younger brother Ian (centre), riding in a lower division for Swindon.

Speedway was always a serious business on track but off duty there was always plenty of time for fun. Tamworth and Southampton made a short tour to Italy in September 1949, riding three matches against each other in Milan, with the south coast side winning the rubber 2-1. Here Tamworth riders Peter Orpwood, Bill Dalton, Steve Langton (partly obscured), Lionel Watling and Basil Harris attempt to cure the pretend air sickness of Southampton man Jimmy Squibb.

New facilities were constructed far down in the south west pensinsula at St Austell in Cornwall, in the Army garrison town of Aldershot, at Rayleigh, on the London-Southend arterial road in Essex, while greyhound facilities were shared at Yarmouth on the Norfolk coast, and at Swindon and Oxford.

The pre-war venue at Brandon, on the Coventry to Rugby road, utilised by the Army during the war years, was returned to its owners and the nissen huts and other military buildings adapted as refreshment facilities.

A track was carved out of heathland near Ipswich and, as a final and, as it turned out, a rather belated expression of speedway's post-war expansion, a new facility was built in the south coast seaside resort of Weymouth.

At the same time racing, usually on a Sunday, continued at fairly primitive pre-war venues such as Eastbourne and Rye House in Hertfordshire, with these two circuits joining together in 1954 with California (Little California in England, near Reading), Ringwood, in the New Forest, and Brafield, on a former midget-car circuit in Northamptonshire, to form the Southern Area League.

If a new promoter could convince the Control Board of his suitability and financial status, he then faced the problems of laying or restoring a track surface, building a safety fence, pits and dressing rooms as a minimum investment, and ensuring that there was enough public transport to get his spectators to and from the meetings, at a time when private car ownership was limited and petrol was rationed.

Returner number one: Bill Kitchen was back in action after World War Two, but at Wembley not Belle Vue as top riders were initially pooled for the re-start of league speedway.

(Right) Returner number two: another rider resuming activity after the hostilities was Australian international Bill Longley, here enjoying some assistance in the pits.

A would-be promoter in fact faced what was described at the time as 'a terrifying array of obstacles to overcome' before he could present his first meeting. Bureaucracy in the late 1940s was still rampant in a country where strict control had become an acceptable norm in wartime.

Anyone wishing to open a speedway track needed to consult not just the local council where the venue was located, but also the Ministries of Health, Town and Country Planning, Works, and Transport.

Major Bill Fearnley, secretary of the Control Board, at times appeared taken aback by the number of people who believed investing their capital in speedway promotion was a justifiable risk. He went on record in 1949 as saying he personally would not consider speedway promotion without capital of £10,000 – the equivalent today of more than a million pounds.

The tracks were an obvious essential for the sport's expansion, but so was an adequate flow of riders skilled enough to put on a level of racing that justified charging admission.

This in itself was a very significant issue in 1947, when the creation of Division Three meant the need for at least a pool of eighty riders, given the likelihood of injuries and other factors, to sustain a league of eight tracks. With the majority of the starters little more than raw novices, coming from hastily-formed training schools, it put a huge onus on those responsible for the training to produce men almost instantly capable of giving the public value for their money.

The response from the speedway authorities was well co-ordinated. The former West Ham captain Harold 'Tiger' Stevenson was enabled to set up training schools in the

(Left) Pre-war veteran Phil 'Tiger' Hart inspired Birmingham in the 1946 Northern League.

(Right) Harry Edwards, seen after his transfer from Belle Vue to Norwich, took his place in speedway racing after surviving the horrors of a Japanese POW camp.

winter of 1946-47 at Birmingham and Bristol. When the schools were advertised, Stevenson received a phenomenal 14,000 applications within a three week period. Stevenson later recalled:

> Imagine my dilemma! However, when further enquiries were made and the replies were vetted, a huge job in itself, we found that the age of the applicants ranged from 13 to 48 and included two women. The problem gradually solved itself.
>
> The two tracks used, Birmingham at 402 yards and Bristol, tight and tricky at just 290 yards, were purposely chosen for their differences, to prevent the trainees from become one-track minded.
>
> Backed by the determination of the lads involved and their ability to stick at it, the results exceeded my greatest expectations and certainly made a third division a reality for 1947.

In addition to the products of the Tiger Stevenson training schools, other factors allowed a necessary influx of riders into the sport for the second post-war season. At the top of the game, improving travel conditions meant that in 1947, Harringay, the one member of the London big-five to be absent in the previous year, was able to build a side virtually consisting of returning Australians.

Commonwealth riders, from not only Australia but also increasingly from New Zealand and to a lesser degree from South Africa and Canada, plugged many of the gaps and provided many great crowd-pleasers. In addition, some of the men who had decided not to return to speedway immediately after the war changed their minds when they saw the great success the sport was enjoying.

The Division One clubs, actively talent-scouting at the training schools and on the nation's grass-track circuits, quickly placed the cream of the crop on contracts, and in many cases those who made an immediate impression at the new Division Three circuits were soon snapped up by higher league sides.

What motivated this huge new crop of post-war speedway riders? Glamour, which speedway certainly possessed in huge quantities in those days, and a desire for adventure arising out of a reluctance to settle down too quickly after wartime experiences, played their part.

Money too, was certainly a major factor. Speedway, from its very earliest days, was seen by the majority of riders as a way of earning a good living. That is not to ignore the pleasure competitors took from the actual racing, or from the sport's lively social life, but just recognises the reality.

In 2011, looking back on a distinguished 50-year career in speedway as a rider and manager, that took in the latter part of the period covered by this book, the President of the World Speedway Riders Association (WRSA), Eric Boocock, recalled:

> To me, whatever success may have been achieved, such as winning the British League title in 1966 with Halifax, it was still just my job. It was a business. I don't ever remember turning down a booking to ride in my life, even if it was a busy week.
>
> You ride speedway for one reason and that is to make a living. That is why everyone goes to work.

The best insights into the reasons for riding speedway naturally come from the riders themselves, as in the respected and undoubtedly down-to-earth case of Eric Boocock.

The reasons for taking up the sport, quoted by some of the men who came into speedway racing in the 1940s, vary considerably, as one might reasonably expect.

Some had nurtured a long-term ambition to become a speedway star. Reg Duval, whose career was to take in Liverpool, Coventry, Oxford and Bradford, had been enthralled by racing at Harringay pre-war and had immediately switched his ambition

Post-war discovery one: Glasgow discovery 'Atomic' Tommy Miller was the track's response to Edinburgh's nurturing of World Champion Jack Young.

At the other end of the country, Buckinghamshire farmer's son Ron How starred for Harringay *Racers*, later becoming an international with Wimbledon, before helping Oxford to win the 1964 National League title.

Leicester *Hunters* in 1949, l-r, Jack Baxter, Harwood Pike, Vic Pitcher, Ron Wilson, Cyril Page, Jack Winstanley, John Carpenter and Ernest Palmer.

from being a racing car driver to being a speedway ace. He kept the ambition alive during speedway's long wartime absence and during his National Service, spent largely in Palestine in the mid-1940s.

Reg Fearman, who rode when he was under-age and received his racing licence on the centre green at West Ham on his sixteenth birthday, later going on to a career as rider, promoter, and international team manager, was brought up in a speedway-mad household. His parents were not only regular attenders at their local track, taking their children with them when speedway resumed after World War Two, but also provided a home during the season for visiting riders from Australia – a natural motivation for Reg.

Others were talent-spotted as they rode in amateur grass-track meetings, often opposing established speedway stars such as Jack Parker. A good performance would bring forth the suggestion that they seek a trial in professional speedway, and many careers began this way.

Wembley's Arthur (later Sir Arthur) Elvin determined to make the post-war *Lions* an all-English side, and his assistants combed the grass-tracks for talent, unearthing future World Champion Freddie Williams, from South Wales, and subsequently his brother Eric.

Literally hundreds of would-be riders made a bid to break in to the sport in the immediate post-war period, often investing the whole of their demobilisation gratuities into buying a machine and leathers. Some succeeded, some decided it was not for them after experiencing the ups and (often painful) downs of speedway. An unlucky few lost their lives, as the test of controlling a powerful, fast-accelerating motorcycle on a tight bend proved (sometimes almost instantly) to be way beyond their capabilities.

Although many of the men who entered speedway in the immediate post-war era had relatively brief careers, some of the other entrants of the period were, unknown to themselves at the time, to go on to play vastly influential roles in the development of the sport.

The first major British star to emerge after the post-war revival was a gritty north-easterner called John Walter Denton Oliver – 'Dent' Oliver, as he was swiftly christened by his mentor at Belle Vue, 'Uncle' Bob Harrison, pre-war *Aces* star and later team manager at Hyde Road.

Dent Oliver, persuaded to try out in novice races at Hyde Road in 1945, as Belle Vue began to prepare for the return of peacetime speedway, enjoyed a fairly rapid rise to the top of the speedway tree in the sport's golden age.

He won an immediate place in the *Aces* National League line-up in April 1946, and was soon followed by ex-RAF ground crew member Louis Lawson, who had been talent-spotted by the new Belle Vue captain, Jack Parker, while both were riding in a grass-track meeting in the Bristol area.

The Warren family prepare to leave Birmingham for Australia in September 1955. Graham Warren had been a diminished force since sustaining a fractured skull in New Zealand in January 1951 but was still a firm favourite with the *Brummies*. A further accident in July 1955 hastened his decision to retire. Pictured are Graham and wife Pam and children Leigh and Kym.

Eyebrows had been raised in speedway during the post-war pooling operation, when the *Aces'* manager, Eric Spence, had reportedly declined the opportunity to choose his pre-war star Bill Kitchen and had instead plumped for Parker, whose previous experience had been with tracks in the Midlands and London, notably at Harringay.

Kitchen moved on to become a star at Wembley, and as part of the dominant *Lions* side to subsequently to win more National League titles than his rival Parker at Belle Vue. Parker had the edge over Kitchen when it came to individual track success, both in the individual Match Race Championship, which Jack held so frequently that it became known as 'Parker's Pension' and in the initial British Riders Championship and the subsequently revived World Championship.

Oliver developed quickly in an *Aces* side led by Parker, with the strong backing of pre-war Hyde Road star Eric Langton, who had initially retired, only to return and insist on riding for no-one but Belle Vue, driving a horse and cart through the pooling system.

In his first season Oliver scored a highly respectable 76 league points, then more than doubled his haul in 1947. Dent's league form stabilised in 1948, with his runaway success in the Manchester test match, scoring an 18-point maximum against Australia, reflecting the fact that he was generally more at home on the Hyde Road circuit than on away tracks.

In 1949, he scored 363 league points at more than nine a match, sandwiched in the Belle Vue averages between Jack Parker and Louis Lawson, who had made giant strides to catch up with his fellow 1946 starter. Oliver appeared in the revived World Final, which brought great success for England, with Belle Vue's Parker and Lawson finishing second and third behind Wembley's Tommy Price, but the night was not memorable for him personally, at least not in the right way. He failed to score, after being excluded in his first ride.

Dent Oliver's career faltered at a stage when it looked as though many of the richest prizes within the speedway world was in his grasp. He became one of many riders to be caught between the glamorous lure of a sport he could not totally abandon and the desire, particularly strong in a clear-headed and unostentatious man who had known hard times in his childhood on a Northumberland farm, to create and maintain a successful business.

He found league points a little harder to come by in 1950, although his second World Final appearance brought including a race win. At the end of the season Oliver, building up a plant hire and haulage businesses, retired, only to make a comeback, on loan from the *Aces*, at Bradford.

In 1952 Oliver rode half the season for Belle Vue and half for the Bradford *Tudors*, with a virtually-identical points haul and match average at each club. The following year he rode just a dozen league matches for Odsal, and then called it a day.

Dent came out of retirement again in 1956, riding nine meetings for Bradford, then quit again. He surprised the speedway world by re-emerging in 1963, some way past his 40th birthday, to help out Sheffield *Tigers*. His final rides were back at Belle Vue, when he appeared once again in the *Aces* team in 1965.

Yet although his riding days were now over, arguably his greatest contribution to speedway racing was yet to come. As speedway manager at Belle Vue, charged with restoring the club's fortunes after a period of struggle, he drew on his riding experiences – and particularly his knowledge of the difficulty many young men faced in breaking into speedway – to create a production line of successful young riders, including a future English World Champion, Peter Collins.

In contrast to the determination shown by some of his counterparts, often from an early age, to break into speedway racing by any means possible, John Carpenter drifted into the sport almost by accident, and drifted out again in much the same way.

After an adventurous World War Two career in the Royal Navy, including D-Day service on a motor torpedo vessel, Carpenter found himself, like so many others of the period, at a loose-end in his native London. John recalls:

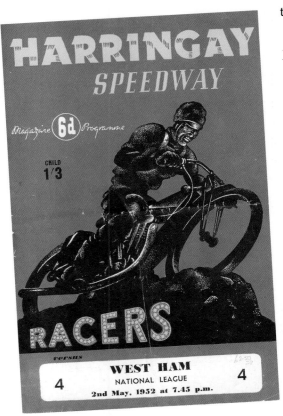

The Harringay programme cover was one of the most distinctive in the sport in the early 1950s, with the illustration based on a sculptured image of a rider.

> I was asked by a friend if I would like to go to Wembley for the speedway. I found myself right at the top of one of the stands and, to be honest, I didn't think very much of it. From where I was standing the riders looked very small and just seemed to be circling around the track without doing a great deal.
>
> I changed my mind when two men in front of me started talking during the interval about apparently how much money the riders could make. This sounded more like it!

After practice sessions at Rye House, John was able to find rides in Holland, racing in front of big crowds for teams including the Holland *Lions* (the *Leeuwen*) and the *Windmolens* (*Windmills*), earning money and gaining experience.

He eventually linked with Leicester, where manager Squib Burton provided a new engine, to be paid for out of John's first earnings. When his frame broke in half and was replaced, he found himself on effectively a completely new machine.

> I started flying then and had a good couple of years at Blackbird Road, where I met and married my wife. She and her friends used to stick a pin in a team photograph and then hope to meet the rider they had chosen. She thought I was tall, dark and handsome from the picture, but when she met me she discovered I had been standing on a petrol can at the time it was taken.

Although many speedway riders revelled in the glamour that surrounded the sport in the days of big crowds and extensive media coverage, John was never comfortable in the limelight, and his wife liked it even less.

> Riders were a real target for the young women supporters and even in those days, there were plenty of people willing to stir up trouble. You only had to be seen signing an autograph or talking to a young person and the poison pen letters would start to arrive. That was something my wife just could not cope with.
>
> I drifted into speedway accidentally and even while I was enjoying success on the track, I was never a great one for watching others race. You could never have called me a fan. So when I lost my team place, I retired to concentrate on the business I had started selling and erecting sectional buildings.
>
> Leicester made several attempts to get me to return, but that was that as far as speedway and myself were concerned.

A more traditional note was struck by the Coventry programme cover for the midland track's 1950 campaign in the National League Division Two and the Kemsley Cup.

Few riders can point to as painful a route into a successful speedway career as Londoner Eric Hockaday. Hammersmith-born Eric began as a fan, dashing home from school each Thursday evening for just long enough to collect the cash to watch Tommy Price, Bill Kitchen and the other Wembley heroes of the era.

His own first venture into racing came through the medium of cycle speedway and in 1949 Eric won the Thames Valley championship. The 'skid-kid' variation of the sport satisfied him only for a while, and the search for funds to buy a real speedway equipment became his priority. That was where the pain came in.

> The money looked like being a big problem, until I met a former rider from pre-war days, Bill Degan, who had been with Plymouth and Middlesbrough. He was at the time running a motor-cycle stunt outfit called Hells Angels, and he suggested I join up to earn the cash for a speedway bike.

Eric soon settled into the routine as the stunt men travelled through the country performing at carnivals and other events. Riding up see-saws, through flaming hoops and up a ramp and across the prone body of a colleague sprawled across a table became a way of life.

Bill Degan, like all good showmen, was constantly on the look-out for a new thrill for the crowds. He devised a new trick which involved the rider, dressed only in bathing trunks, boots and a crash helmet riding up a ramp, into space and straight through a sheet of plate glass. Eric explained:

> The other members of the Hells Angels drew the line at this immediately, but Bill Degan and myself did the act twice daily. The impact smashed the glass completely and the tiny shards used to go into your skin and really sting. After each performance the ambulance men used to bathe the cuts with iodine, so you can imagine that I really earned the money.
>
> On one occasion a bigger piece of glass caused a considerable cut and I needed medical attention. The doctor who treated me told me that if the glass ever pierced a particular artery near the heart, that was the end of me, full-stop. That was when I decided I had enough cash to have a go at speedway, which seemed a lot safer!

His first attachment was to Aldershot, when the Tongham track operated under an open licence in 1953. Eric's introduction to the sport continued to have its pitfalls, with the track at the home of the Shots, which he described as being 'pear-shaped', ensuring that his introduction to competitive speedway racing was a tricky one.

With the sport contracting in the mid-1950s, Eric's apprenticeship was to prove a long one. Compared to his northern counterparts, getting a regular ride was relatively easy, and the Southern Area League, formed in 1954, provided a great deal of enjoyment and individual championship success, if not a lot of actual prize money.

Speedway was just a part, albeit an important one, of activities at Belle Vue, which boasted the title of Showground of the World.

Chapter seven

SURVIVAL OF THE FITTEST

Staying afloat in the turbulent 1950s

When the number of speedway tracks in Britain went into steep decline in the 1950s, the large number of young men still trying to break into the sport went to extraordinary lengths to realise their dreams. Today they still recall the many good times they experienced, alongside the inevitable struggle to make the grade.

AS BRITAIN'S speedway venues shrank rapidly from a post-war high of 37 tracks in 1951, the decline was much more marked in the northern half of the nation.

A disastrous 1954 season brought an end to league racing in Scotland as far as the 1950s were concerned, with Glasgow White City, Edinburgh and finally Motherwell following Glasgow Ashfield into at least temporary oblivion.

Newcastle, Middlesbrough, Hull, Sheffield, Liverpool, Fleetwood, Stoke, and other venues north of the River Trent had also failed over the years, due to a lethal combination of decreasing attendances and a continuing high rate of entertainment tax, which successive governments stubbornly refused to reduce where speedway was concerned.

Of the eighteen tracks that started 1955 in Divisions One and Two of the National League, just two were in the north, at Belle Vue, Manchester and Odsal, Bradford. With eight tracks having disappeared between the start and finish of the 1954 season, speedway now had a glut of riders and there was a domino effect which knocked many experienced performers over and out of the sport.

Top riders from the failed Scottish and northern tracks moved south, particularly to the midlands. Reg Fearman, allocated to Leicester by parent club West Ham after the closure of Stoke, found himself slipping down the rankings within the *Hunters* side as first Ken McKinlay arrived from defunct Glasgow White City and then Ron Phillips signed on from Motherwell. Reg said:

I could see the writing on the wall. The top riders were joining the tracks still running and those riders who were lower down the teams in Glasgow, Motherwell and Edinburgh would all soon be out of a job. I reasoned that it wouldn't be too long before I would be out of a job at Leicester as well.

That wasn't much of a prospect, especially as I was newly married, and so my wife and I set off for a new start in New Zealand.

Southampton and Exeter enjoyed contrasting fortunes as the 1950s progressed and survival became the keynote for much of speedway. The West Country side drifted out of league racing temporarily at the end of 1955 while the Saints eventually became part of the single division National League in 1957, remaining there until the stadium closed for redevelopment at the end of 1963. The riders are Goog Hoskin of Exeter on the outside and Brian McKeown of Southampton.

With riders as experienced and successful as Fearman believing their future in British speedway was bleak, the outlook for the newcomers who resolutely refused to abandon their dream of breaking into the sport was starting to look exceedingly grim.

Speedway had become a regional, not a national sport, concentrated in London and the south of England, where Wembley, West Ham, Wimbledon and Rayleigh kept the flag flying, in the midlands and central England, where Birmingham, Coventry, Leicester, Oxford and Swindon were operational, in East Anglia, with Ipswich and Norwich, and over a broad swathe of the south-west, where Southampton and Poole, Bristol, Exeter and (for a short time only) Weymouth were racing.

Young riders in the south and central part of the country, apart from varying opportunities at the National League tracks, also had the benefit of the semi-professional, mostly Sunday afternoon circuits comprising the Southern Area League.

The north of England was a different matter altogether. For a good part of the 1950s training and the occasional competitive speedway opportunity was available at a rough

Rye House – this is the original track in the early 1950s with a corrugated iron-clad safety fence, remained a prime route into speedway for aspiring young riders throughout a difficult decade. Here John Carpenter, later of Leicester, is in the lead.

and ready track in the Newton Heath area of east Manchester, run by former Fleetwood rider Ernie Appleby. Many bright prospects graduated from there, with Ernie's help, to Belle Vue.

Later in the decade, novices desperate for a chance to prove their worth could choose between three widely-differing but highly individualistic career paths.

They could take a trip to the coast and defy high tides, sea mists and other hazards to practice, and occasionally compete in organised matches, on the vast and bleak stretch of sand which bordered the Irish Sea at Ainsdale on the Lancashire coast.

They could stay at home and ride in a now legendary series of hotly-contested handicap races, improbably named after an American fairground ride, staged at Belle Vue.

Alternatively, they could acquire a passport, hop across the English Channel and throw in their lot with a madcap circus troupe of speedway riders and stuntmen, who toured the backwaters of rural France, and presented a hair-raising version of the sport like nothing ever witnessed before or since.

Ainsdale Sands had been used for many years for unofficial training by individual rider. Eventually the owners were persuaded to legitimise the practise and set aside an agreed area for speedway.

North-western novice Lew Grepp recalls travelling from his home south of Manchester to Ainsdale in the mid-1950s.

Lew had been a spectator at Belle Vue for many years and was also a keen competitor in cycle speedway league. Unlike Newton Heath, which had a properly laid-out track and a safety fence, Ainsdale was simply what it said on the can, a beach. Lew explained:

> Ainsdale was different every time I went there. A lot depended upon the tide.
> Sometimes the sand we rode on would have a deep surface and at other times it
> would be quite slick. It was very unpredictable and the best you can say is that it

Eric Hockaday, a product of California in the Southern Area League, who also enjoyed National League racing with Coventry in the 1950s, made his first public appearances on a motor bike as a stunt rider.

gave you experience of riding in the different conditions you were likely to find on a proper track.

Ainsdale did host organised speedway matches, certainly against the Newton Heath training track, and Liverpudlians Peter Craven and his elder brother Brian used the beach for practice.

Much of the activity at Ainsdale took place during the winter months and in addition to keeping an eye on the encroaching tide, riders also needed to be wary of the sea mists that could blow in quickly and lead to a potentially dangerous lack of visibility.

The importance of the Southern Area League in keeping the interest of young riders in the south of England in the latter part of the 1950s cannot be over-emphasised. That importance was recognised by National League promoters including Wimbledon's Ronnie Greene (right) who is pictured presenting the California Championship to Eric Hockaday.

Option number two for aspiring novices was Belle Vue. When Belle Vue speedway manager Johnnie Hoskins introduced a new handicap race for novices, he adopted the name probably inspired by a fairground ride called the Bubble Bounce, which tended to throw its less fortunate patrons on to the floor of its teacup-shaped cars.

Lew Grepp, who rode in bubble bounce events along with a large number of other young hopefuls, explained that the experiences of the riders matched those of the patrons of the fairground ride:

For me, the bubble name came from the bubbling enthusiasm of the young riders. The bounce was inspired by the way we would regularly fall off our machines and quite literally bounce off the Belle Vue track and safety fence.

To maximise opportunities for the novices queuing up for rides at Belle Vue, the bubble bounce races, held in the second half of the meetings after the league or cup matches, were contested by five, and sometimes six, riders. A couple would start from scratch, at the starting gate, with the rest staggered at intervals behind.

Another regular competitor in the bubble bounce was Yorkshireman Tony Robinson, who also graduated to racing at Belle Vue after learning how to control a speedway bike at Newton Heath. Tony recalled:

> I remember the bubble bounce as being really hairy. You took your life in your hands just going out on the track, because none of us really knew how to ride properly. It was all a question of trial and error.
>
> In those days no-one really gave us any help or advice. The only time I can remember anything being said about the way I was riding was when new Zealander Ron Johnston, the Belle Vue captain at the time, talked to me in the pits.

Lew Grepp, Tony Robinson, and several other bubble bouncers eventually gained team places with Belle Vue or other league sides. Other contestants were part of the Hyde Road scene for varied lengths of time, before disappearing from the speedway picture. Both Grepp and Robinson, despite the bruises from the bouncing aspect of the event, the lack of advice from the management or the more senior riders on techniques or on how best to tune and set up their machines, remember the bubble bounce as being great fun. As Tony Robinson concluded:

Eric Hockaday's team-mates during his 1950s spell with the Coventry *Bees* were a mixture of local midland products and men from farther afield. Pictured l-r are Les Tolley, Reg Duval, Per Olaf Soderman of Sweden, team manager Stan Williams, Hockaday, the injured Charlie New of New Zealand, local boy Jim Lightfoot, Bob Mark from Scotland and Nick Nicholls.

Breaking into speedway has never been particularly easy. For youngsters in the north in the 1950s it was really hard. The bubble bounce might have been a bit of a free for all, but it gave inexperienced riders, absolute beginners really, the chance to race on a great track in front of big crowds. We learnt a lot and we certainly had a lot of fun.

An early bubble bouncer was Ted Connor, who had been spotted by Belle Vue in 1954, riding in a scramble at Carnforth in Lancashire. The Manchester track also ran Monday evening training sessions, where some of the novices were, not to put too fine a point on it, extremely raw. Ted explains:

Belle Vue's Harold Jackson, who helped with the training sessions, used to lean on the safety fence while the novices were out on the track. You were supposed to watch him closely, as he was pointing the directions we needed to take.

When I first went to Belle Vue, one of the track's greatest pre-war stars, Eric Langton was also involved in running the training school. Eric asked me to go out and show him what I could do. The first time I came out from the starting gate I walloped the fence on the first bend and I thought I had blown my chance. Eric said no, have another go, from a rolling start this time. The result was the same, wallop in the fence again. Unbelievably Eric's response was simply to say, 'you'll do for me!

Riders in the north relied heavily on the training track at Newton Heath near Manchester and on practice on Ainsdale Sands. Tony Robinson, pictured here, rode at both venues and was one of the legendary Belle Vue bubble-bouncers. The reward for his persistence both sides of completing his national service was a team place for the *Aces*.

The highest profile casualty of speedway's 1950s slump was the iconic Wembley *Lions*, who withdrew from league speedway after the Empire Stadium's managing director, Sir Arthur Elvin, a great champion of the sport, died in early 1957. Here is a Wembley line-up in somewhat happier times, back row, l-r Freddie Williams, Eric Williams, Jimmy Gooch, Eric French and team manager Duncan King. Kneeling (left) is Brian Crutcher and right Trevor Redmond, while skipper Tommy Price is on the machine.

Ted believes the bubble bounce handicaps in particular were exciting for the spectators because of their sheer unpredictability, and kept the interest going into the second halves of meetings.

No-one ever knew what was going to happen, who would fall off and who would actually finish the race, There was great rivalry but at the same time a great sense of friendship among the novices, and you would allow another man to ride your bike if anything went wrong with his.

Ted Connor was one of the riders who also took the option of crossing the channel to ride for the Victor Boston speedway circus troupe. He returned from his adventures as French Champion, a title that still ensures his place in the record books today.

Victor Boston usually employed two British riders only with his troupe, and as the 1950s were coming to an end Ray Day and Tommy Roper from Bradford took the ferry to Calais in Ray's pick-up truck.

Brian Crutcher, who joined Wembley from Poole for the 1953 season was speedway's golden boy of the era – in this case literally, as the holder of the British Match Race Championship Golden Helmet in 1956, Wembley's final season of league racing of the era.

Tommy's experience as a motor mechanic served the Bostons well, as the lorry in which the troupe moved from village to village, carrying speedway bikes, personal belongings and the family's animals, including cats and hens, regularly had gearbox trouble. Ray Day explained:

> Victor Boston, who kept Tommy and myself waiting in Calais for a couple of days before sending us the money to travel down to Grenoble to meet up with the troupe, wanted us to sleep in the lorry as well, but we weren't having that and insisted that he put us up in small hotels.
>
> Boston would contact the mayor of each little town or village and get him to find a field where we could stage a meeting. It wasn't speedway at all, just riding around in a circle really, but most of the villagers who turned up to watch had never seen anything like it anyway.
>
> We used to ride our speedway bikes, no brakes of course, down to the village cafés to publicise the meetings. We didn't often get paid, but at least we had a good laugh.

While the northern novices were enjoying the sea air at Ainsdale, all the fun of the fair at Belle Vue, and the pleasures of rural France, the Southern Area League provided a bona fide experience of competitive racing.

Although speedway racing at Brafield was short-lived, midland novices were well catered for at Coventry, where promoter Charles Ochiltree had a genuine belief in encouraging young talent. Many of the riders who made up his teams in the 1950s, and on into the 1960s, were Coventry born and bred, including Jim Lightfoot, Peter Brough, Derek Tailby, Johnnie Reason and Les Owen.

All had been carefully nurtured at Brandon, largely through the Ashlawn Trophy, run in the second halves of meetings, which produced a flow of riders for the *Bees* team. Not all the riders looking to compete in Brandon second halves could get as much racing

While the juniors (and some who had been established team men before the mid-1950s slump) struggled for rides, National League speedway continued. Adopted New Zealander and twice World Champion Ronnie Moore of Wimbledon (left) leads Kiwi Ron Johnston, the captain of Belle Vue.

as they wanted however, such was the competition and two in particular, Peter Gay and Bill McGregor, were also drawn to join the Victor Boston troupe in France.

Speedway, despite all the odds, was alive and kicking in the mid and late 1950s. There were always promoters, usually current or former riders, prepared to open up closed venues, often risking their savings and acquiring a few grey hairs.

From 1954 up until the birth of the Provincial League in 1960, at least sixteen tracks staged challenge matches and individual competitions after closing their doors to league speedway. It was not regular league racing, but it kept the sport at least faintly alive in areas where it could have died completely.

One alternative for young British riders desperate for some form of racing in the later 1950s was to join the Victor Boston circus, which took speedway to many parts of rural France. In this shot Coventry juniors Peter Gay (left) and Bill McGregor watch as Boston's son Claude, who rode speedway himself, entertains the crowd at the interval on one wheel.

The racing in France was wild and woolly, with the riders competing on surfaces varying from grass to pebbles dredged from a river, with the occasional meeting in stadia as grand as the velodrome in Lyon. Here Peter Gay and Bill McGregor get in some practice in the long grass!

The established riders of the era, with team places secure, were able to enjoy life in the sport. Here Ron Johnston of Belle Vue and Ronnie Moore of Wimbledon previously pictured fighting it out on the track, entertain a fur-bedecked 'starlet' – one of the many to present awards at meetings in that period.

There was not always a great deal of official encouragement for those outside what some saw as the magic circle of the National League.

In 1957, former Liverpool star man Reg Duval decided to re-introduce the sport to his old home at the Stanley Stadium on Merseyside. With the rate of entertainment tax at last reduced, he believed he was on to a good thing.

I had reckoned without the attitude of some of the established National League promoters, who effectively decided what happened in speedway. Running open meetings and challenge matches, I was dependent upon using the riders they had under contract. It was alright at first but eventually they started to make life difficult.

I think they believed they had kept the sport alive through the hardest times and they didn't think it was right for someone to come in when things were improving and do well. The fact that I was providing rides and reviving the sport in one of the country's biggest cities didn't seem to matter to them. They just wanted to protect their own interests.

The tide really started to turn for speedway as a whole in 1959 when, perhaps, television had started to lose some of its novelty value.

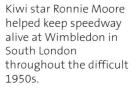

Kiwi star Ronnie Moore helped keep speedway alive at Wimbledon in South London throughout the difficult 1950s.

Chapter eight

REVIVAL IN THE AIR

The neglected north leads the way

Speedway racing was very much alive and kicking in the late 1950s. Although some London-based journalists had forecast its complete demise following the closure of Wembley for league racing, the tracks that survived attracted healthy crowds, while the period saw the rise of a generation of legendary riders. The sport was surviving, but it was not thriving, as it had a decade earlier. Then, to the surprise of a great many people in the sport, the first signs began to appear of a widespread revival in interest, which was ultimately to lead to the creation of an exciting new league.

T HE ALMOST miraculous expansion of speedway racing in Britain at the end of the erratic decade of the 1950s had its origins in one of the most unlikely settings imaginable for any kind of renaissance. Equally, the revival was driven by the efforts of a most unexpected saviour.

The forlorn district of Moss Side in south Manchester, notorious for gang warfare in the last decades of the twentieth century, still screams out for its own resurrection, despite the huge sums of money spent in recent years to improve the quality of life.

The area provided a home and business opportunities for the man who some regard to this day as the long-term saviour of speedway racing in Britain. Mike Parker, usually described in fairly vague terms as 'a Manchester businessman' was not even really a speedway person. Those who knew him at the start of his involvement in the sport in the late 1950s describe him variously as a jobbing builder, and a demolition contractor.

He ran a hardware store in Moss Side and lived, at least for part of the time, in a flat above the shop. He certainly also owned property in the area.

His initial contact with speedway came through Belle Vue where the constant search to add novelty to speedway second halves had led *Aces* manager Johnnie Hoskins, already responsible for introducing stock car racing to Hyde Road, to include races for midgets, or speedcars, in the programme.

It was to this obscure shop and flat that a variety of established speedway people were to find their way, as Parker sought to become involved in reviving the sport in the north of England, where by 1958 Belle Vue was the sole regular venue.

The Moss Side gatherings were not in fact the first stirrings of speedway revival in the late 1950s. What was to become a major expansion of the sport through the formation for the 1960 season of a new competition, the Provincial League, can probably trace its roots back to the appointment, in 1957 of a new Conservative prime minister.

Harold Macmillan combined Old Etonian social graces with a populist instinct that recognised the British public's hunger for a better, if more materialistic lifestyle.

He believed that one way to increase prosperity was to ease the burden of taxation. His administration finally abolished the entertainment tax that had helped to drive speedway to its knees.

This prompted several attempts, mostly by former riders, to revive speedway at closed tracks. In 1957 and 1958 Geoff Pymar and Cyril Roger at Exeter, Reg Duval at Liverpool, Trevor Redmond at St Austell and former Glasgow promoter Ian Hoskins at Motherwell ran short seasons of racing, with mixed success.

Parker and others wanted to go a step further than merely staging brief programmes of challenge matches and individual events, useful though these were in providing additional bookings and cash for riders, and for keeping the speedway flame alive in some of the more distant venues.

In the final years of the '50s, life began to stir in centres where speedway had seemed dead and buried, particularly in the very parts of the country where the mid-1950s slump had hit hardest, in Scotland, the north, the midlands, and in the former hotbed of the west country.

A cast was slowly being assembled of men who believed speedway was again ripe for expansion. At the start, their individual plans and schemes were not only uncoordinated, but included some vastly different ideas of how to bring about the speedway renaissance. The story of how these eventually coalesced into the Provincial League, despite at best cynicism and at worst direct obstruction from the speedway establishment, is a fascinating one.

The National League promoters, dominated by Ronnie Greene of Wimbledon and Charles Ochiltree of Coventry and Leicester, were proud – and justifiably so – of the role they had played in keeping speedway alive through the slump.

From their respective power bases at Brandon and Plough Lane, they had

History in the making. A rare picture of one of the pirate meetings promoted by Manchester businessman Mike Parker, in 1959. This is at Cradley Heath in the Black Country and shows The Midlands against Liverpool *Pirates*. The Liverpool riders are Ted Connor (left), who was instrumental in getting together riders to race for Parker that year, and Roy Peacock. The Midlands riders are unknown.

watched as major venues, which in their day had attracted huge crowds in both London and the provinces, had gone to the wall.

The drawback was that something of a siege mentality had entered the fortress that was the

surviving British speedway empire. Greene and Ochiltree, together with the highly-professional businessmen who ran Belle Vue, Manchester, and their fellow promoters at the other surviving National League venues, were prepared to support a certain amount of limited growth within the sport, but were understandably cautious and suspicious of false dawns.

The months between Christmas and a new season at Easter can be cruel for speedway fans. It was in the late winter of 1957 that Wembley withdraw from league racing after the death of Sir Arthur Elvin. In contrast, February 1959 brought a hint that the speedway establishment itself was preparing to abandon its attitude of out-and-out caution and extend feelers beyond the strongholds that had survived the mid-decade meltdown.

Speedway Star carried a claim that the National League promoters were reported to be interested in re-opening – for non-league racing – centres including Bristol, Wolverhampton, Sheffield and Cradley Heath. The rumours of new tracks for 1959 started to become a reality on March 27, when former Wembley star and World Finalist Trevor Redmond re-opened the doors at Plymouth's Pennycross Stadium.

The rotund and enthusiastic New Zealander had found it difficult to find a riding niche in speedway after the closure of Wembley, where he had spent six seasons in the *Lions'* team, after serving a two-season apprenticeship at Division Three Aldershot. For a time it seemed likely that promoting, at St Austell and elsewhere, would see his virtual retirement from the saddle.

The first 1959 meeting at Plymouth saw the home side lose out by 49 points to 47 to a team labelled as The Midlands. The two sides comprised a mixture of big names and journeymen riders, either contracted to National League teams, nominally retired, or hovering on the fringes of the sport.

The re-opening was a success, with a reported attendance of 10,000, which all helped to sustain Trevor Redmond's dream of a Western League, with the *Devils*, St Austell, Exeter and Bristol competing.

Bristol returned in early July 1959, with a 52-38 victory for the home side over a Swedish touring team. The pattern of composing a side for the re-opened track out of top National League riders continued, with Belle Vue's Peter Craven representing the local *Bulldogs*, along with one time Bristol stars Dick Bradley, now with Southampton, and Johnny Hole.

Ted Connor, a former scrambles rider from Lancashire, became the effective leader of the northern junior riders in 1959, helping to form an Independent Riders Association – the name was changed from Independent to Unattached when someone realised the initials read IRA! Ted (right) is speaking to Bill Bridgett, the grass-track ace who rode speedway for Stoke and later became Mike Parker's right-hand man at Wolverhampton.

The tentative steps taken at Plymouth and Bristol were soon overshadowed by the news that Johnnie Hoskins, manager of Belle Vue since 1953, planned to re-open one of the London Big Five circuits, at New Cross.

The closure of the *Rangers* mid-season in 1953 had been a bitter blow to speedway's prestige and the announcement that Hoskins was prepared to have another go was a major morale booster.

The 'Frying Pan', as the Old Kent Road track was affectionately called, re-opened on August 19 1959. The *Star* reported an attendance of more than 10,000 spectators, including many newcomers to speedway.

The racing surface was in poor condition, which led to plenty of incident to keep the crowd concentrating. It was reported that one perplexed rider inquired how best to get around the track in the prevailing conditions and was told:

> Get in that big rut near the starting gate and stay in it all the way around. It's just like
> a tramline.

The 1959 meetings at Plymouth, St Austell, Bristol and New Cross had a common theme. They were all taking place with the complete blessing of the Speedway Control Board and of the National League promoters, and were providing additional bookings and earnings for a fair cross-section of riders.

Things were also stirring in the north of England, but here not only the circumstances of the revival, but also the attitude of the speedway authorities, was different.

Scotland's first speedway meeting since Ian Hoskin's brief revival at Motherwell two years before took place on April 18 1959 and provided one of the sport's rarest occurences. The Engineering Society of Edinburgh University promoted a meeting in aid of student charities, won by Doug Templeton, a former Glasgow Tiger, who had ridden at Motherwell during the brief Hoskins revival in 1957.

Mike Parker now came into the brightening speedway picture. Through his midget car connection with Belle Vue – he drove in the meetings as well as owning the cars – he became aware of the large pool of northern novice riders, whose opportunities were at present confined to second half rides at Hyde Road – when they could be fitted in – and practice on Ainsdale Sands.

Parker asked one of the Belle Vue hopefuls, Ted Connor, who was to play a crucial role in the developments surrounding a new league, to gather together riders for planned meetings at Liverpool and Bradford.

At first, Parker played it strictly by the book, applying to the Speedway Control Board to run mixed speedway and midget car meetings at Stanley Stadium, Liverpool and, in partnership with Jess Halliday, at Bradford's Odsal Stadium.

The application was rejected. Parker, no respecter of authority, decided to go ahead anyway, and with rides particularly hard to come by in the north, there was no shortage of riders willing to compete incognito or even to risk their ACU licences by appearing in the programme under their real names. Ted Connor explained:

> You have to remember that it was extremely difficult to try and break into speedway at this time and we in the north of England did not have the advantage of the Southern Area League.

Revival was truly in the air at the turn of the decade and former Birmingham captain and later team manager Phil 'Tiger' Hart revived the *Brummies* at Perry Barr. He is seen testing son John's new machine. John became the last ever rider to lap the original Perry Barr track in 1960.

Responding to the feeling of renewal, former *Brummies* rider, test star and World Finalist Graham Warren returned to England from Australia in 1959 to ride for Coventry and is pictured on his return getting acclimatised to the British summer at the Southampton track. When Phil Hart ran a season of challenge matches at Birmingham the following year, Warren wore the *Brummies* colours again.

At Belle Vue it was like having to pull the short straw to get a ride. The Control Board and the ACU did absolutely nothing to help us. We were desperate for more competitive speedway and so you can imagine that when Mike Parker came along and offered us rides at tracks he was planning to re-open, we jumped at the chance, illegal or not.

I put the group of willing riders together, and because we were riding without Control Board and ACU permission, which excluded us from getting any help or indeed recognition from the Speedway Riders Association, the SRA, we formed our own organisation, which we originally called the Independent Riders Association

When we realised what the initials were we changed it pretty quickly to the Unattached Riders Association!

In addition to Jess Halliday at Bradford, Parker was also joined by the Jephcott brothers from Cradley Heath and interest was also shown by former Stoke rider Don Potter, who was ambitious to promote at Wigan.

The northern and midland 'pirate' meetings were largely successful and Ted Connor has little doubt about where much of the credit lay.

Mike Parker for me was the absolute saviour of speedway. He paid very fair rates for points and starts, almost double what the boys in the Southern Area League were earning, and just as importantly for the riders he paid full insurance costs for the riders. A meal was provided for us all after each of the meetings he promoted.

The Bradford v Liverpool clash in July 1959 – Bradford winning 41-30 – saw the Odsal side feature riders such as Ray Day and Tommy Roper, among the many who had ridden for the Boston organisation in France in a bid for competitive speedway, together with Stan Holey, Vic Lonsdale and Norman Redmond, who was also later to play an important part in the formation of the Provincial League.

Liverpool staged the return fixture on July 29, when Bradford again took the honours, winning 42-29.

The Mike Parker initiative was being noticed throughout the country. In the south, the Southern Area League, revived after a blank 1958, was enjoying a solid season. Its five teams, Eastbourne, Yarmouth, Aldershot, Rye House and Ipswich, managed to complete the league fixtures and this stability prompted the promoters at the member tracks to consider expansion for 1959.

Belle Vue continued to thrive throughout speedway's ups and downs. Although the 1950s, unlike the '30s were barren for the *Aces* in terms of National League championship success, they virtually monopolised the Britannia Shield three years out of four when it was staged as an addition to the league programme in the 1957-1960 period. L-r Graham Coombes, Bryce Subritzsky, Dick Fisher, Tony Robinson, Ron Johnston, Bob Duckworth (partially hidden), Arthur Wright and Peter Craven.

Collectively, the Southern Area League promoters, with the assistance of journalist John Wick, who was the secretary of the organisation, began to consider an expansion that would include the Parker interests in the north.

The SAL men found Parker willing to listen to their ideas, despite his apparent scorn for the Control Board, its methods and its personnel. Wick was advised to negotiate with the Board's chairman, Lt Colonel Vernon Brook, and to his delight, the response was encouraging.

This was not the last time that Brook, who had been associated with speedway since its inception in Britain, was to display an unusually open mind for a speedway administrator and play a significant and beneficial role in the affairs of what was to become the Provincial League.

A meeting at the Control Board's offices proved positive and the authorities decided that they were prepared to sanction the formation of the new competition.

Although the powers-that-be in the National League, and many in the speedway media continued to be sceptical, planning for a new competition started to accelerate and it seemed as though everyone was likely to benefit. Sadly, no scenario is ever perfect, particularly in speedway, and there were eventually to be losers as well as winners.

Aldershot was run by John Pilblad, a lifelong speedway fan who came into speedway promotion almost by accident, while at the same time pursuing an increasingly successful career as a top television outside broadcast cameraman.

The two separate camps, SAL in the south and Parker and his associates in the north and midlands, started exploratory talks. John Pilblad remembers:

I was telephoned in 1959 by Mike Parker, who asked me to go up to Manchester to talk about possible mutual interests.

When I arrived at his base in Moss Side, the first thing I noticed was Mike Parker's midget cars, all on a low-loader, just parked out in the street outside his shop and flat. He had bought every car he could lay his hands on and effectively ran midget car racing, such as it was.

In later years, given the neighbourhood, obviously these would have simply disappeared or been destroyed on the spot but at the time no-one seemed to touch them.

I had been a speedway fan since 1949, seeing the sport for the first time in my home town of Leicester, when the *Hunters* were launched in the National League Division Three. After national service in the RAF I was accepted as a technical assistant in the BBC's Outside Broadcasts section in 1954, and started to watch the sport at Wimbledon and West Ham.

At Plough Lane I used to stand with a group of enthusiasts called the Ferndown Flyers, who once a year were allowed by promoter Ronnie Greene to ride in a special second half event. One of them told me that the stock cars were pulling out of Tongham Stadium at Aldershot and I was persuaded to re-open the track for Southern Area League racing.

As word spread of the plans being hatched, many more expressions of interest in the new league flowed in. Former riders Wally Mawdsley and Pete Lansdale applied for Rayleigh, whose last season of National League racing had been in 1957, Frank Varey joined in with Sheffield, and the Jephcotts made an application for Cradley Heath. A further feather-in-the cap of the Provincial League organisation came when the new management at Poole, led by the experienced Charles Foot and Jack Knott (of the Southampton family) threw in their lot with the new competition for 1960.

Mike Parker also looked at Sun Street Stadium, in Hanley, together with former Potters skipper Dave Anderson, another former rider anxious to become reconnected to speedway. Parker approached another ex-Potter, Reg Fearman, who also travelled to Moss Side for a meeting at the hardware store.

During the lean years the *Sunday Mirror* newspaper continued to support speedway when others dropped away. Here the paper's sports editor George Casey presents a trophy to Leicester skipper Ken McKinlay.

The outcome was that Fearman agreed to join forces with Parker at Stoke, not only promoting at the track but also acting as rider coach. The Parker/Fearman liaison was to become one of the real powerhouses behind the success of the Provincial League, although when it turned sour – Fearman eventually winning a legal battle over a bitter dispute between the former partners – it at one stage threatened to tear the league apart.

Despite the success of negotiations for a new league, one stumbling block remained, over the

Eastbourne, spent most of the classic era primarily as a Sunday afternoon training track. The Sussex circuit's application to join the new Provincial League in 1960 was rejected by the Speedway Control Board. Pictured, L-r, are Bob Dugard, John Dugard, Dave Still, Charlie Dugard, promoter and the father of Bob and John, Bob Warner, Gil Goldfinch and Colin Goody. Skipper Frank Bettis is on the machine.

position of the northern riders who had joined Parker and staffed his meetings at Bradford, Liverpool and Cradley Heath.

Here the key man proved to be the secretary of the Speedway Riders Association, the freelance journalist Cyril J Hart. He was sent north to a meeting with the northern riders at the Corporation Hotel in Manchester, with a clear remit from SRA chairman Cyril Brine of Wimbledon to hammer out a deal.

Ted Connor and Norman Redmond believed a compromise might be possible which would see the Unattached Riders Association affiliate to the SRA. Hart ruled out that

Also rejected by the Control Board as Provincial League members were Aldershot. Shots promoter John Pilblad turned his attention to promoting non-league at Weymouth but the headaches continued. In this case the wayward tractor used to prepare the track at the Dorset holiday resort is the cause of his exasperated expression.

The JAP engine dominated speedway for many years, through the 1950s, when this advertisement appeared in the sport's media, through to the middle 1960s.

possibility, but then changed the entire tenor of the meeting by offering to appoint one of the Unattached men as an official SRA representative, to look after the interests of the riders in the north.

The Unattached Riders Association members, after inviting Hart to step outside while they considered their decision, agreed to come back into the official fold. Ted Connor was appointed as the SRA northern representative on a show of hands, and the last obstacle to the Provincial League had been removed.

Although the powers-that-be in the National League, and many in the speedway media continued to be sceptical, planning for a new competition started to accelerate. There were, however, at least a couple of final stings in the tail.

The Control Board vetoed membership of the new league for Rye House and Eastbourne, on the grounds of the difficulties of racing on a Sunday. John Pilblad's application for Aldershot was also rejected, on the grounds that the support for SAL racing at Tongham in 1959 had been insufficient to meet the additional expense of a nationwide league.

Pilblad was granted a licence for open meetings, but admits today that the rejection for the Provincial League still hurts.

On the rider front, when the news of the agreement reached between the SRA and the northern-based riders reached the Control Board, it was decreed that bygones should be bygones, and any racing licences suspended should be restored – except in one case. Ted Connor recalls:

Everything was legalised again after the meeting with Cyril J Hart. The Provincial League was accepted, but with the exclusion of Ted Connor. I was to be made a scapegoat because of my leading role in helping Parker to find riders for the 'pirate' tracks and also because I had dared to ride in those meetings under my own name.

Thankfully for me, Mike Parker put his foot down and said, 'no Ted Connor, no Provincial League under the Control Board,' because of that I was able to race at Stoke in the league's first season.

Despite the heavy blow of his application for Aldershot to join the new Provincial League being rejected, John Pilblad nevertheless ran open meetings at the garrison town track. Here Ken Mellor (left) and Aldershot team-mate Ted Spittles are on the outside of Ipswich's Dennis Day.

Some of the National League's hopefuls compete at Southampton in July 1960. L-r Ken Mellor Southampton, Len Silver (Ipswich) , Peter Vandenberg (Southampton, obscured), and Colin Goody of Ipswich.

For some of the men involved, notably Reg Fearman, Mike Parker, Ian Hoskins and Trevor Redmond, the Provincial League was to prove the start of long and distinguished careers in promoting and managing speedway.

For others like Pilblad, after being involved in the initial planning, there was to be little but heartbreak. Veteran rider and promoter Charlie Dugard at Eastbourne recovered best from the initial blow, although it took another decade before Eastbourne was finally welcomed into the league structure the track had quit after a single post-war season in 1947 (amazingly, crowds were insufficient at Arlington Stadium despite the Eastbourne team winning the first-ever Division Three title.

Once little more than a Sunday training track in a field, Arlington, thanks to the efforts over the years of the Dugard dynasty, is now a well-developed stadium with an Elite League team and a superb racing surface looked after by Bob Dugard, one of Charlie's sons.

The emblem of the Aldershot *Shots* is worn by Ken Mellor in June 1960.

The speedway media's initial attitude to the moves which led to the formation of the Provincial League was as cautious as that adopted by the National League promoters. There were suggestions that having a nationwide league with tracks stretching from Poole to Edinburgh was biting off more than the new competition could chew, and regionalisation was suggested.

One leading columnist described the proposal to go ahead with one competition as 'possibly suicidal'. Speedway at the higher levels, both within its administration and its media, perhaps understandably given the sport's chequered history, was institutionally and instinctively inclined to err on the side of caution.

Happily for the future of the sport, Parker, Fearman, and the rest of the men behind speedway's brave new world had the courage to launch a venture which overnight in the winter of 1959/60 doubled the size of the sport's league structure.

Chapter nine

SPEEDWAY RENAISSANCE

The Provincial League to the rescue

If the advent of the Provincial League in 1960 saved British speedway from stagnation, it was a case of history repeating itself. The original 1930s Provincial League allowed the sport to strike out again from its last ditch strongholds in the metropolitan areas. The 1960s version proved an often controversial competition which, although proving the driving force behind a speedway renaissance, eventually split the sport into two bitterly-feuding camps.

A declining National League and a desperate shortage of opportunities for riders to enjoy their speedway and at the same time earn enough money to at least pay their way. A group of promoters re-opening defunct tracks to form a viable second tier league and encourage new talent, yet initially encountering opposition from an entrenched and suspicious speedway establishment.

A familiar scenario? It corresponds both to the situation in speedway at the end of the 1950s (as described in the previous chapter) and also to the state of affairs existing more than 20 years previously, in the winter of 1935-1936, when the original Provincial League was born. Speedway's fortunes truly do run in cycles.

The 1960 Provincial League had aims in common with its earlier incarnation. At its core was the ambition to restore speedway to some of its most far-flung outposts, while at the same time providing competitive league racing for riders unable to find places in the elite National League sides. Pay rates, as in 1936, were intended to be modest.

Fans watched team-building plans for the new competition with great interest. When the new league was first mooted, many in positions of authority saw it simply as a geographical expansion of the Southern Area League, where spectators had essentially enjoyed a leisurely Sunday afternoon's racing, often in pleasant surroundings.

Liverpool, one of the tracks which staged unlicensed meetings in 1959, was one of the founder members of the Provincial League for the following season. Here the *Pirates* line up at Stanley Stadium for an early match against the visiting Stoke Potters.

When the new league's membership for 1960 was finalised, it included Bristol, Bradford, and Rayleigh, tracks which had seen racing at the highest level. It also included Poole, where the management had decided to step down from the National League. The patrons of these tracks were clearly going to expect to see something more than worthy SAL-type competition, almost exclusively featuring junior riders.

The fact that the Control Board had turned down applications for PL membership from Aldershot, Eastbourne and Rye House, meant Yarmouth, another venue with a not-too-distant history of National League Division Two racing, was the only former SAL team confirmed in the new league.

A Liverpool team picture in 1960. The *Pirates* rarely tracked the same team in consecutive matches.

The Board's actions meant that the PL was to be a entirely different animal from what a great many commentators had originally envisaged.

Some tracks initially remained faithful to the concept of tracking teams of novices, stiffened by one or two experienced men acting as a rider/coach, but it quickly became obvious that the majority of spectators were demanding something more for their admission money.

From the start, the three teams that were to dominate the initial Provincial League, Rayleigh, Poole and Bristol, ensured that there was plenty of experience in their line-ups. The effects of the two-tier recruitment policy were felt immediately.

Good Friday, April 15 1960, saw the first two matches in the new league, Rayleigh versus Cradley Heath and Stoke v Liverpool. Bristol should also have staged a match that night, against Poole, but the meeting was rained off.

Rayleigh had built a team chock-full of experience. Pete Lansdale, co-promoter with Wally Mawdsley at the Essex track, Alan Smith, and Reg Reeves had bags of National League Division Two experience and Eric Hockaday, although an SAL product, had considerable experience of National League racing with Coventry.

It was no doubt sheer coincidence that pitted experienced Rayleigh against a Cradley side largely comprising trainees from a winter school. The inevitable mismatch occurred and Rayleigh piled up 50 points from the 12 heats that constituted the initial PL format, against Cradley's 20.

At Stoke, the teams were only slightly better balanced, and the result was a resounding 44-26 win for the more experienced home side. The *Potters* had two riders from the

The Provincial League brought together experienced riders and young hopefuls. Pictured left to right is Belle Vue junior Jim Yacobi, who had a few outings in the new competition in 1960, with Jack Winstanley, one of the men who had struggled to find regular rides in the mid-to late-1950s and often rode abroad, and Guy Allott, who was allowed to step down from National League Leicester to PL Sheffield in 1961. Allott was seriously injured when he fell from the tractor during a victory parade in March 1963 and slipped under the track grader. The occasion was a Sheffield v. Belle Vue challenge match.

Sheffield's Owlerton Stadium is packed for an early Provincial League match with the *Tigers* racing against the Edinburgh *Monarchs*.

In the first season of the Provincial League Sheffield relied heavily on their loan riders from National League Belle Vue. Tony Robinson (right), Jack Kitchen (left) and Robinson's 'dope and oil boy' Kev Meehan have a technical discussion on the subject of tyre cutting.

Len Silver, who had fought hard to retain a foothold at National League Ipswich during the 1950s, quickly became a Provincial League star at Exeter. Silver, with his arm in a sling after breaking a collarbone in his first away match for Exeter at Rayleigh in 1961, was a great favourite at the County Ground with the crowd and the ladies of the Supporters Club, led by secretary Mrs Winifred Kerr (left). Silver won the Provincial League Riders Championship in 1962 and led the *Falcons* to a Knock-out Cup victory.

Tony Robinson, one of the first stars of the Provincial League, won and then held the league's individual match race championship, the Silver Sash, until injury prevented him from defending the title. Here he is helped to adjust the sash by Sheffield promoter and pre-war Belle Vue star Frank Varey and a niece of Varey, who had presented the award.

side's Division Two days in top scorer Ray Harris and Reg Fearman and the promising Peter Kelly also did well. Stoke at least initially fulfilled the promise to include some of the northern riders who had struggled for a place in speedway during the later 1950s, with team places and points for Gordon Owen, Arthur Rowe and Ted Connor. Liverpool owed the relative respectability of the scoreline to the reasonably experienced Brian Craven, elder brother of Peter, although the novice Roy Peacock weighed in with six points.

As the season progressed teams which had started out with a good contingent of novices had to strengthen or face the prospect – and the potential consequences at the turnstiles – of regular crushing defeats.

The initial Provincial League proved to be a series of competitions within a single league. Rayleigh had sent an immediate message to the opposition that the club's experienced side would take some beating and Bristol and Poole had also assembled strong and experienced teams from the start.

The *Bulldogs* were built around two men with extensive National League Division One experience in the early 1950s, former Wembley man Trevor Redmond and Johnny Hole, a member of the Bristol side during its spell in the top tier. Poole welcomed back to racing Ken Middleditch, another man with experience at the highest level, and he was later joined by other experienced *Pirates* like Tony Lewis and Norman Strachan.

Predictably, Rayleigh, Poole and Bristol contested the league honours among themselves, the *Rockets* and the *Pirates* each finished with 32 match points, each side

One former National League second string and reserve with Wimbledon who found success in the Provincial League with Newcastle *Diamonds* was Gil Goldfinch, a Southern Area League discovery. Goldfinch was runner-up in the Northern Riders Championship and is pictured with winner Tony Robinson of Sheffield.

Basking in the reflected glory of Silver Sash and Northern Riders Championship victories is Tony Robinson's fiancée and later wife Doreen Powell, sister of Belle Vue rider Bill Powell.

losing just two of its 18 league matches. The *Rockets* took the honours on superior race points. Bristol lost three matches and finished third with 30 points.

The respectable middle group consisted of Sheffield, Stoke and, rather surprisingly, Cradley Heath. Such success as Sheffield enjoyed was largely due to their loan riders from Belle Vue, Tony Robinson and Jack Kitchen.

Stoke's initial blend of experienced riders and novices changed as the season progressed and the strength of some of the opposition became more apparent. Ray Harris and Reg Fearman were joined by former team-mates Les Jenkins and Ken Adams, who was signed from National League Oxford in one of several transfers from the top tier allowed by an initially reluctant Control Board.

Cradley stayed mainly faithful to the men who had started off the season, and Eric Eadon in particular did well, enjoying his best speedway campaign ever and averaging

The Provincial League brought speedway back to Scotland, with the Edinburgh *Monarchs*. This line-up from Old Meadowbank shows, left to right, George Hunter, Wayne Briggs, Willie Templeton, Alf Wells, Jimmy Tannock, promoter Ian Hoskins and Ken 'Casper' Cameron. On the machine is Monarchs skipper Doug Templeton.

more than seven points a match. Team manager Phil Malpass, a former *Heathen* himself, pulled off a master stroke by signing former Dudley Wood team-mate Harry Bastable, a rider with Division One experience at Birmingham who had been out of favour latterly at Leicester.

Just below this group of teams were Yarmouth and Edinburgh. The east coast side saw Ivor Brown, another Leicester rider who had spent many years on the sidelines at Blackbird Road, come through to become one of the new league's greatest success stories.

In Scotland, with Ian Hoskins at the helm at Old Meadowbank, Edinburgh, the crowds turned out to watch a team of mainly Scottish riders. Jimmy Tannock, Jimmy Cox and Doug Templeton had seen their budding careers cut short by the demise of speedway north of the border some years before, while George Hunter had been the main discovery when Hoskins operated Motherwell in 1957.

Undoubtedly the single biggest name to appear in the Provincial League in 1960 was that of Ron Johnson, the Scottish-born former Australian test star and New Cross rider who attempted yet another comeback at Old Meadowbank. Sadly, Johnson, now in his 50s and racked by the effects of his many injuries, failed to score in his five matches.

The final group comprised Liverpool and Bradford. The Merseyside *Pirates* struggled to win just four matches, while the hapless Odsal-based *Panthers'* record was one victory and 17 defeats. Liverpool had many talented riders but no-one of any consequence was able to ride in more than half of the team's league matches.

Cradley Heath, which had staged a pirate meeting in 1959, also became Provincial League founder members. Unlike on Merseyside, the crowds flocked to the Black Country track. This 1962 line-up shows, left to right back row, Derek Timms, George Bewley, Ivor Brown, Harry Bastable, and John Hart, with Stan Stevens and Ivor Davies kneeling.

Brian Craven averaged 11 points a match from his nine appearances and Belle Vue man Bryce Subritzky was only just a little behind. Another *Aces* loanee, Jim Yacobi, scored nine points in his one appearance for the *Pirates*. Pre-war veteran Wal Morton and junior Dennis Jenkins recorded the highest number of appearances (12) but there was no real consistency at Stanley Stadium – 22 riders used in league matches – and sadly, too few spectators.

Bradford used 18 riders in the quest to find a winning combination, but this eluded them. They had little luck, losing the experienced Des Haswell after he had averaged more than eight points in four matches, and the team was kept afloat mainly by the efforts of Tommy Roper, a future star with Belle Vue, and by fellow Yorkshireman Ray Day, who at away matches often had to also act as team manager for the *Panthers*.

The Bradford management attempted to follow a path which became increasingly well trodden during the season, and sign an experienced man from the National League. Eric Boothroyd, who lived in Halifax and was struggling to make much of an impression at Leicester, would have been ideal but in this instance the Control Board, still at least theoretically wedded to the concept of a league for novices, refused to ratify the move.

When the first season of the PL came to be summed up, it was seen as a substantial success, although a surprising one in some ways. A high league position was not always reflected in the attendance figures. Big crowds were attracted to Stoke – some 11,000 for the opening Good Friday meeting – and gates were excellent too at Edinburgh, despite the lack of track success, at Bristol, Poole, Cradley Heath and Sheffield.

The most telling crowd statistic of all was the chilling fact that rock-bottom Bradford, with just one win to the team's credit, had a higher average gate than champions Rayleigh.

The *Rockets'* management may have been able to display the Provincial League trophy at the end of the season, but their balance sheet was a disaster. Runaway victories at The Weir had seen crowds gradually decrease week after week, evidence yet again that the magic formula for speedway success demands that a winning team is not too strong to exclude the prospect of reasonably close racing.

As far as individuals were concerned, the experienced men inevitably headed listings. The top ten compiled by *Speedway Star's* commentators at the end of the season was composed of five men with some National League Division One experience, and three others who had been prominent in the old Division Two.

The top ten had just two men who could be described in any way as newcomers. Tony Robinson, in third place in the *Star* ratings, held the PL's Silver Sash until forced to concede the honour when injury prevented him from defending the title, and he also beat an experienced field on his home track at Sheffield to win the Northern Riders Championship.

The Provincial League introduced a 'quick death' knock-out cup, with the rounds and semi-finals conducted over just one leg. Bristol beat Rayleigh 100-89 on aggregate in the two-legged final.

The Provincial League Riders Championship (the first winner in 1936 had been former Wembley man George Greenwood, riding for Nottingham), was held at Cradley and won with a maximum by the vastly-experienced Trevor Redmond. Not all the PL tracks held qualifying rounds, some nominating riders for the final.

After the season closed, one of the men involved in the birth of the Provincial League, Charles Foot of Poole, summed up the season. He couldn't resist a jibe at those in the

Wolverhampton won the 1963 Provincial League championship but promoter Mike Parker refused to allow his team to be promoted into the ailing National League, sparking the speedway civil war which saw the Provincials run 'black' outside the Control Board jurisdiction the following year. Three of the younger Wolves riders, Rick France, Dave Hemus and James Bond celebrate the victory.

The National League still had ten tracks during the inaugural Provincial League season. This group of riders includes Australian star Aub Lawson, once of West Ham and latterly of Norwich *Stars*. Lawson retired at the end of 1960. Also pictured are, left to right, Ken McKinlay of Leicester, Peter Moore (Wimbledon), Bert Edwards, Phil Clarke (Norwich), Peter Craven (Belle Vue), Per Olaf Soderman of Coventry, Aub Lawson, and Harry Edwards of Norwich, brother of Bert.

sport's governing bodies and those commentators in the media who had doubted the ability of the new competition, given its considerable geographical spread, to survive, let alone flourish.

In the early 1960s, despite the wave of support for the Provincial League, the National League featured classic racing between the world's finest riders, including, as pictured here, Ove Fundin (leading) of Norwich and Bjorn Knutson of Southampton.

Did some of the know-alls in speedway journals have a time forecasting doom and failure! The league has been successful everywhere, some tracks better than others, but every promoter is satisfied to go on next year. At Edinburgh, Sheffield and Stoke the crowds have averaged between 6,000 to 10,000 – figures which many National League promoters just dream of. Poole had its 'stand full' notices out several times during the season.

Why is this the case? Why did Major Fearnley, the secretary of the Control Board say in his programme notes for the Riders Championship final: 'If I want thrills I go to see Provincial League racing.'

In at the birth of the Provincial League, Ted Connor (left) and Peter Kelly ride for Stoke at Bradford in 1960.

The answer was given by Cyril Hart, the secretary of the Riders Association in the same programme. 'What's the word to describe Provincial League racing? Unpredictable – and that is the keynote of its success.'

Foot said the PL had been criticised in some quarters for bringing back 'old stars', but the truth was that the experience of these riders had helped bring on the novices.

> If you had been in the pits with me you would have seen with wonder and admiration the care and instruction given by the likes of Ken Middleditch, Johnny Hole and Trevor Redmond to the young riders they regarded as their protégés.

Charles Foot was not one hundred per cent accurate in his prediction that all of the ten founder PL tracks would re-emerge for 1961. Liverpool's crowd levels had been poor and the management pulled the plug, Yarmouth also decided that racing in such a widespread league was uneconomic, Bristol's Knowle Stadium was sold for development, and Bradford failed in time to achieve a move from the cavernous Odsal to a more compact home at Greenfields in the city.

The loss of four tracks – 40 per cent of the new league's membership – could well have been a disaster, and would have proved the dismal jimmies of the media to have been right in their prediction that one big league with no regional split could prove to be 'possibly suicidal.'

Is that really what I said? Peter Kelly of Stoke studies the programme notes, watched by Ted Connor (left) and Arthur Rowe (centre).

What saved the day was the Provincial League's amazing ability, which was to endure throughout its five seasons of existence, to annually not only replenish but usually add to its membership. If tracks closed, fair enough said the PL promoters, we have more waiting in the wings to take their place.

So it was that for 1961 the six continuing teams from the initial PL season were joined by no fewer than five newcomers. There were speedway revivals in the West Country, with Plymouth and Exeter building on open licence seasons to commit to league speedway, and in the North-East, with the return of Middlesbrough and Newcastle. The fifth revived track, Wolverhampton, paved the way for hard-fought and well-attended local derby matches between the Monmore Green *Wolves* and Cradley Heath.

Poole made no mistake in winning the 1961 PL title, with Plymouth taking a surprising but well-merited second place. The four other debutants finished in the last

A full house at Sheffield for a challenge match against National League Belle Vue watches the riders leave the starting gate.

four positions in the table but, as at Edinburgh the year before, a lowly finish did not mean poor crowds.

Experienced men continued to dominate the scorers, with the Cradley duo of Ivor Brown and Harry Bastable both notching more than 400 points in all matches raced under the Provincial League banner. Graham Warren, the golden boy of both the Australian test team and Birmingham *Brummies* in the late 1940s, before serious injury blighted his career, had a new lease of life at Wolverhampton, averaging more than ten points a match in league fixtures, while the likes of Clive Featherby at Sheffield and Doug Templeton at Edinburgh surged into the top ten scorers.

In individual competition Ivor Brown and Eric Boothroyd, who had eventually been allowed to move down a league and join Middlesbrough, both held the Silver Sash match race championship through four challenges. The number of individual riders to hold the title over the season, a dozen, showed that there were few foregone conclusions in the PL.

Cradley Heath won the Provincial League Knock-out Cup, beating Edinburgh in the final, and Reg Reeves lifted the Riders Championship title, ahead of 1960 winner Trevor Redmond, and Morrie Mattingley of Plymouth. The final, which in 1961 saw qualifying rounds at each of the PL's 11 tracks, was staged at Harringay.

Fans at Yarmouth and Bradford were not entirely deprived of speedway, with open-licence racing taking place there at a Provincial League level, and St Austell and former Southern Area League tracks Eastbourne and Rye House also operated during the season.

The 1962 season saw the Provincial League expand to 13 tracks. Rayleigh, where a 1960 championship title and a respectable 1961 fifth placing failed to attract sufficient support, dropped out, but Bradford returned (at Greenfield) and there were two particularly interesting newcomers.

For the initial PL season Poole had successfully negotiated a step down the ladder from the National League, and had proved a powerhouse at this level. After the Leicester *Hunters* had endured a torrid season in the top flight in 1961, Blackbird Road's owners, Midland Sports Stadiums, granted the right to stage Provincial League speedway for

A close-fought midlands derby match between Stoke and Cradley Heath in the Provincial League, with Cradley's John Hart on the inside.

the new season to Mike Parker and Reg Fearman.

Despite the team's struggles, National League crowds at Leicester in 1961 had averaged more than 3,000, and these were expected to largely stay loyal despite the drop in status. It was not to be, the '*Young Hunters*' as the team was named struggled throughout the campaign, crowds dipped on occasions below the four figure mark and the promotion, in the words of Fearman, a former Leicester rider, 'haemorrhaged money'.

STRICTLY NO BETTING

DUDLEY and BARBARA McKEAN—
"A Merry Monarch and His Queen"

Photo by Edinburgh Evening Dispatch

SATURDAY, 4th MAY 1963 at 7.15 p.m.
Provincial League Match
MONARCHS v. LONG EATON
CONTROL BOARD LICENCE No. 63/9   A.C.U. PERMIT No. SP 927

Rayleigh v. Long Eaton
Saturday, May 25th
at 7.15 p.m.
OFFICIAL PROGRAMME — PRICE 9d.

Edinburgh promoter Ian Hoskins used some of the glories of Scotland's capital (the Sir Walter Scott Memorial in this case) to illustrate his programme cover in Provincial League days and marketed an evening at the speedway as an integral part of a visit to the Athens of the North.

(Right) In a more modernistic spirit (for the times) Rayleigh had a space age theme in keeping with the team's *Rockets* branding.

Only Bradford, who won just five of the team's 12 home matches, finished below Leicester.

The other intriguing event of the 1962 PL season was the return of speedway to Wales after an absence of almost a decade. Trevor Redmond introduced the sport to Neath, to a primitive arena close to the ruins of town's abbey. On the track, the *Dragons*, with an exciting but publicity-shy Australian newcomer called Charlie Monk, were sensational, finishing runners-up to Poole.

Off the track, the crowds were poor, not helped at one stage by an epidemic that broke out in the town, and towards the end of the season Redmond staged some of the *Dragons* league fixtures at his non-league track at St Austell.

Ivor Brown topped the Provincial League scorers for the second consecutive year, followed by the vastly experienced Boothroyd, Guy Allott and Jimmy Squibb – all former National League riders. The top five was breached however by young Australian Geoff Mudge, a true product of the new league.

Individually, the Silver Sash was initially the story of two men. Ivor Brown of Cradley, fast becoming *the* rider to beat in PL circles, looked to be establishing domination with six straight wins. His record was eclipsed by Tony Lewis of Poole, who beat Brown on the Cradley rider's own track at Dudley Wood and then went on to defend the title on an amazing ten occasions.

At the end of the season Len Silver, an outstanding success at Exeter, ended the season in possession of the Silver Sash, snatching it from the up and coming Roy Trigg at the County Ground and then defending it on six occasions, including a walkover at Stoke.

Silver finished top of the individual heap in more ways than one in 1962, winning the Provincial League Riders Championship, staged for the first time at Belle Vue and leading Exeter to a Knock-out Cup victory over Stoke.

The 1963 season was to prove an extremely mixed campaign for the Provincial League. It was the year the PL lost its innocence, when the smouldering resentment of the National League promoters finally burst into flames.

Plymouth, Neath, Leicester and Bradford quit at the end of 1962 season. Yet again, the promoters came up with replacements and there were a record 14 starters for 1963. The Neath team, as expected, switched to St Austell, giving Cornwall league speedway for the first time since 1953. Rayleigh returned, two London sides were admitted in the shape of Hackney Wick and New Cross (making the Provincial in the league title somewhat ridiculous), and Long Eaton, lost to racing in any form since 1954, came in under the control of Reg Fearman.

During the winter of 1962, the business relationship between Mike Parker and Reg Fearman deteriorated sharply, over the issue of the leases for the tracks at Wolverhampton and Newcastle. The dispute threatened the 1963 Provincial League season and in February of that year, the Provincial Promoters Association was warned by Speedway Control Board secretary Major Bill Fearnley that unless the matter was speedily settled, the Board would refuse to licence the five tracks Parker and Fearman

One of the men to blossom into a heavy-scoring star in the Provincial League, first with Yarmouth and then with Cradley Heath, was Leicestershire sub-postmaster Ivor Brown. Everything about Brown screamed style, from his immaculate riding gear to his technique.

Raymond Arthur 'Billy' Bales was an England international and World Finalist who loyally served Norwich *Stars* for 13 seasons until the track closed in 1964. He then saw out the rest of a distinguished career with Sheffield *Tigers*.

controlled between them. The threat energised the lawyers, and a settlement was reached which favoured Reg Fearman.

The 1963 season itself was generally successful, although the latest and last attempt to restore speedway to New Cross failed miserably. Promoters Mawdsley and Lansdale, so successful at Exeter, were unable to generate any enthusiasm for PL racing among small and apathetic crowds at the Old Kent Road track, and withdrew mid-season.

The Parker/Fearman rivalry continued on the track, with the 1963 PL title being disputed by Parker's *Wolves* and Fearman's *Potters*. Wolverhampton were crowned as champions ahead of Stoke. The title controversy was, however, as nothing compared to the bombshells which were about to follow.

Although the National League had remained relatively healthy during the first two years of operation of its Provincial counterpart, with ten tracks in both 1960 and 1961, things began to fall apart seriously in the winter of 1961-62. The number of tracks starting the season fell to eight, a situation which worsened when the shaky Ipswich promotion failed and resigned mid-season.

The seven National League starters in 1963, Southampton, Wimbledon, Coventry, Belle Vue, Norwich, Swindon and Oxford, just about constituted a viable competition. To provide extra rides for NL men, Alan Sanderson re-opened Leicester for challenge matches and individual events, but after a reasonable start crowds dropped away badly and the venture flopped.

The Provincial League had begun in 1960 in an atmosphere of suspicion on the part of the National League track chiefs. Opposition turned to a grudging acceptance as the PL proved to be well-organised and professional, although Ochiltree and Greene in particular seemed to resent the fact the upstart new competition was increasingly seen as the more vibrant organisation.

At the end of the 1963 season Bannister Court Stadium at Southampton was sold for redevelopment and it was rumoured that The Firs at Norwich would soon suffer the same fate.

With just six guaranteed National League teams for 1964, and with the prospect of that figure eventually being reduced to five, Ochiltree, Greene and their less assertive but equally determined colleagues elsewhere, still possessing the lions' share of influence with the Board of Control, went on the offensive.

The solution was seen to be a raid on the successful and virtually self-sufficient Provincial League, in search of extra teams to make the senior competition viable again.

The result was speedway civil war.

Chapter ten

SEE YOU IN COURT
Speedway's true men in black

Speedway's historic National League, created in 1932 and at its peak boasting 37 tracks in three divisions, was on the rocks at the end of 1963. The two-year revival of New Cross in 1960/61 and the return of Ipswich from the Southern Area League had produced a healthy membership of ten clubs in that latter year, but it was nothing more than a temporary respite. The efforts by the National League promoters to save their bacon by 'poaching' one or more Provincial League teams led to the PL running on an unlicensed basis in 1964, triggering a dispute which was settled only when one of the country's senior legal figures was called upon to arbitrate.

T HE PROMOTERS of National League speedway in England in the late 1950s and early 1960s were a cautious group of men, who combined an undoubted love for speedway with a hard-headed business approach to the game. They had for the most part watched as so many of their counterparts disappeared during the near melt-down of the mid-1950s, when the lure of television and other consumer-boom home comforts coincided with the continued existence of a vicious rate of entertainment tax.

The Provincial League enjoyed its best season to date in 1963 and even the initially sceptical speedway media had to admit that the new organisation was well-run and provided entertaining racing for a generally enthusiastic public.

The success of the new brand had obviously not gone unnoticed among the ranks of the increasingly embattled National League administrators and it was only natural that there should be some resentment of the newcomer's bright image.

The closure of Southampton at the end of the 1963 campaign meant that the National League's problems were starting to mount up alarmingly. The NL promoters had already suffered a hammer blow a year or so before when Britain had lost its automatic right to stage the World Championship Final at Wembley, a privilege enjoyed each September since 1936 (with the exception of the 1939-49 period).

Pressure had been building for some time from Sweden, an increasingly powerful and influential voice within the FIM, and the 1961 final was held in Malmo. Wembley was the venue again in 1962 and 1963, but the new rule was alternation, and the NL men knew that the 1964 event was scheduled for the Ullevi Stadium in Gothenburg.

Unlike at some other points in its history, British speedway as a whole was not at risk in the winter of 1963-64. The Provincial League was flourishing and, as was to be demonstrated yet again in the run-up to the new season, able seemingly to replenish its stock of tracks almost at will.

What was at stake was the fate of the longest-surviving and most prestigious league structure in speedway, home of the tracks which employed the top British, commonwealth and continental stars, Fundin, Briggs, Ronnie Moore of New Zealand and Peter Moore of Australia, Bjorn Knutson, Nigel Boocock, Ken McKinlay and others.

Who were the men behind the National League, who confusingly for some speedway fans appeared to continue to wield such power and influence in British speedway whilst their organisation was crumbling around them?

Following the end of the 1963 campaign, the rump of six National League tracks included just two of the sport's original top-level teams, Wimbledon and Belle Vue, both of which had been ever-present since the birth of British speedway.

Coventry and Norwich had participated before World War Two, but as league tracks both Swindon and Oxford were essentially post-war creations.

Ronnie Greene, who had the promoting rights for speedway at Wimbledon Stadium, had promoted the sport at Bristol in the 1930s before becoming associated with the South London track.

Created OBE for his wartime service as a senior officer with the fire service in London, he was a formidable character credited by all with keeping speedway alive in the capital city. He had nevertheless offended many would-be promoters, including Reg Duval at Liverpool in 1957 and subsequently, and significantly, Mike Parker. There was a widespread belief that for all his eminence, he formed an obstacle to plans to rebuilding the sport in any meaningful way.

Belle Vue was a special case in virtually every respect. The fact that speedway represented just one activity (albeit an important one) within the overall interests of

The team at the eye of the storm in the winter of 1963-64 was Wolverhampton. Promoter Mike Parker, seen here talking to his Monmore Green rider James Bond, refused to give in to a Speedway Control Board demand for the *Wolves* to be promoted to the ailing National League. Parker won support from his fellow Provincial League promoters for his stance and the PL ran unlicensed in the 1964 season.

the company that ran the Manchester leisure complex, meant that the track always occupied a unique and in some ways privileged position in speedway racing.

After the Iles family ran into financial difficulties, their successors on the board of Belle Vue (Manchester) Ltd, led by Sir Leslie Joseph and Charles Forte, were content to let the speedway managers at Hyde Road provide the public interface, but kept a tight control of policy.

Although Belle Vue in the early months of 1964 appeared to be solidly part of the National League family, there was a suggestion that the variety of opposition offered by the Provincial League on a weekly basis was tempting, at least to the speedway management. The main concern of the Belle Vue directors was not dabbling in speedway's politics, but providing attractive speedway entertainment at Hyde Road on Saturday evenings to help attract patrons to the overall leisure experience. Their stake in the sport was a less personal one than that of Green and Ochiltree.

As it proved, the overall Belle Vue management decided to stay with the National League. Events later in the 1964 season proved however that the directors' primary aim was always the well-being and business integrity of Belle Vue as a whole.

Charles Ochiltree was every inch a speedway man but also every inch a business man.

He was speedway's main thinker and strategist, and his main promoting interest at Brandon Stadium, Coventry, had been a substantial success since its post-war re-opening in 1948.

Ochiltree's acumen was backed up by the wealth of Alan Sanderson, and in the winter of 1963/64 the Midland Sports Stadiums combine controlled Brandon, Blackbird Road at Leicester, currently lying fallow as far as speedway was concerned, a greyhound track at Lythalls Lane in Coventry, and the speedway promoting rights at West Ham Stadium.

In the hot seat at the very start of the 'black' 1964 Provincial League season was Exeter co-promoter Pete Lansdale, pictured with admiring supporters when he retired from riding for the *Falcons*. Exeter staged the first 'pirate' meeting of the year, a challenge match against Cradley, when some of the midland club's top riders were absent, delaying their decision on whether to support the Provincial League.

The latter connection was soon to prove crucial.

A man with a military bearing, who did not suffer fools gladly, Ochiltree had worked his way up the sport's administrative structure, from being a backroom boy at Hackney in the 1930s, and at Harringay in the 1940s, to become higher profile manager at Brandon when the track re-opened in 1948.

His shrewd management, combining equal proportions of showmanship and attention to detail, built a successful team, with impressive attendances enjoying steadily developed facilities, in what is still today the sport's most impressive British speedway arena, if one excludes the one-off Cardiff Millennium Stadium grand prix

One of the riders who decided not to appear at Exeter in the historic first match under the Provincial League Promoters Association regime was Ivor Brown, Cradley Heath's number one. When the return leg of the challenge was raced in the midlands a few days later, Brown signed a contract before the start of the match and returned to the team.

For James Bond, looking forward to just his second season at Wolverhampton, riding 'black' had little noticeable effect apart from being informed that he was now banned by the ACU.

venue. Ochiltree's own personal status advanced as he was rewarded for his success and ability by the millionaire Sanderson.

Ronnie Greene and Charles Ochiltree were by far the dominant figures in the National League world of the time. They were members of the Speedway Control Board and appeared to have the full confidence of the ACU and of the Royal Automobile Club, which was responsible for nominating the lay, or independent members, of the Board.

Their determination to save and maintain a competition which had endured since 1932, no matter how decayed it might have become, was understandable.

A copy of the infamous banning letter sent by the Speedway Control Board to all riders who competed in the 1964 Provincial League.

TELEGRAMS:
"SPEECON," PICCY, LONDON

TELEPHONE:
GERRARD 6664 & 6665
WHITEHALL 7734 & 7735
7735

THE SPEEDWAY CONTROL BOARD LTD.

68 BREWER STREET, LONDON, W.1.
83 PALL MALL, LONDON, S.W.1.
DIRECTORS:
G. R. ALLAN (CHAIRMAN)   H. C. BRINE   E. G. COPE
R. W. GREENE, M.B.E.   C. H. KING   C. E. OCHILTREE   T. E. RYAN   T. REDMOND   K. E. SHIERSON
SECRETARY: MAJOR W. W. FEARNLEY

J. Bond.

10th April 1964

Dear Sir,

A Court of the Speedway Control Board consisting of Mr. G. R. Allan (Chairman), Mr. T. E. Ryan and Mr. H. C. Cornwell sat to-day the 10th April at this address to consider the charge against you under Regulations 57 and 160 for riding at an unauthorised meeting.

After giving consideration to all the evidence it had at it's disposal, the Court found you Guilty and decided that you should be suspended sine die.

Yours faithfully,

Secretary

Perhaps the dominance of Greene and Ochiltree had become so ingrained that they forgot that they had also caused a significant degree of resentment among the men who had built the Provincial League against what at times had been substantial opposition from the sport's establishment.

Confident of RAC backing, the National League now more or less demanded that Wolverhampton, champions of the Provincial League and an extremely successful venue financially, should accept promotion, together with one other track, the identity of which has never been confirmed.

That the champions of the PL, the logical prime candidates for promotion, should be a Mike Parker track, was perhaps unfortunate for the National League men. Reg Fearman, at the centre of the eventual decision to run the Provincial League with or without official backing in 1964, was well aware that there was little sympathy between Greene and Ochiltree and the Manchester man.

> It was Parker's unlicensed meetings at Bradford and Liverpool in 1959 that had set the ball rolling for 1960. I am sure Charles Ochiltree and Ronnie Greene had been very suspicious of Parker and the forming of the PL.
>
> I do know for a fact that Charles Ochiltree never trusted Parker at any time and I am pretty sure that the same went for Greene. Both of them were 'proper' business people with a lot of experience and 'clout' behind them.

On the other hand, Parker certainly owed nothing to Greene and Ochiltree, who had attempted to strangle his northern revival activities at birth. There was certainly no meeting of minds and the stage was set for open hostilities.

Although the stand-off with the National League did nothing to heal the breach between Fearman and Parker, the PL promoters as a whole, once they had decided to resist coercion, decided to stick together come what may. Faced with the might of authority in the form of the RAC and ACU, together with the experience and influence of the senior promoters, they realised that they must hang together or risk losing their financial and emotional investment in the sport.

Riders had decisions to make about whether to stay legal or ride in the Provincial League. Norman Hunter was with Hackney in 1963 but for 1964 switched to the 'official' National League and linked with West Ham, the track re-opened to make the NL viable.

When the PL made clear its intention to operate as normally for 1964, the threats began. Riders warned they would be automatically suspended. It was not an easy position for many. Although it could be argued that men like Ivor Brown owed their new found stardom, after years of struggle, to the Provincial League, they had nevertheless been part of the speedway establishment for a decade or more.

Deciding to ride black would mean a rift with promoters they knew and trusted, and with fellow riders who would stay within the official fold. They would lose their ACU licences, would no longer be included within the qualifying rounds of the World Championship and would probably lose any chance of international bookings.

This was an issue for a number of Provincial League men, notably Jack Winstanley of Newcastle and Ray Harris of Stoke, who had raced on the continent for many years. They would be excluded from any other form of motorcycle racing, and would cease to be members of the Speedway Riders Association.

The ambitious Colin Pratt, with PL Stoke in 1963 (and still involved in the promotion of speedway nearly 50 years after the split) initially decided to stay legal and ride at National League Swindon. Not earning sufficient money at the top level, he joined Provincial League Hackney.

Set against this was the secure position of the Provincial League, which was hardly likely to collapse without official backing, and the need in many cases to simply earn a living. With neither side willing to budge an inch, the crunch would obviously come when the talking stopped and the action began.

The eyes of the speedway world turned towards the County Ground, St Thomas, Exeter, where the first match in the now unlicensed Provincial sphere – the *Falcons* versus Cradley Heath in a challenge match, rather than a full league fixture, was scheduled for Monday 16 March 1964.

As the date got closer, the war of words amplified, with both sides intensifying the arguments.

The Control Board issued a formal warning of suspension to any rider competing on an unlicensed track. Elder statesman Jack Parker, a long-time leading light in the Speedway Riders Association and a legendary name not just to fans but to the new generation of riders, was fielded by the official side in attempt to persuade as many riders as possible to boycott the Provincials. Eric Hockaday recalls:

> Jack Parker was still a big name and very influential in the sport. The Control Board
> and the SRA got him to try and persuade people not to ride in the 'black' Provincial
> League. Quite a lot of people were still uncertain which way to go at this stage.

Len Silver, still simply a rider at the start of 1964 but destined to become a promoter and leading speedway administrator at Hackney later in the season, was captain of Exeter in the run-up to the new season, and took his responsibilities seriously.

As the County Ground fixture approached, he took the opposite approach to Jack Parker. In later interviews, Silver recalled:

> I took it upon myself, as captain, to personally telephone every rider due to appear
> that day and persuaded most of them to ride against the Control Board's wishes.

Monday 16 March was a freezing day, but some 4,700 spectators turned out for the eagerly-anticipated match which saw the Provincial League as a whole, and the fourteen individual riders who went to the tapes, cross the line into open rebellion.

Many of the Provincial League promoters, still at that stage unsure of the support from the riders (and the public) had made the trip to Exeter. The simple fact that a match took place at all, watched by an encouraging crowd, was hailed as a victory for the Provincial League, but the circumstances under which the meeting was run left many questions unanswered.

Although the speedway split could at times be bitter, inter-league friendships between riders persisted across the divide. Here Vic White (left), who was an official of the Provincial League version of the Speedway Riders Association in the 1964 season, acts as spanner man for National League Coventry's Bryan Elliott. The mechanic is Frank Lewin.

The response from the home team to Len Silver's telephone initiative was overwhelming. The *Falcons* were at full strength, despite earlier suggestions that Alan Cowland might decide to stay legal, and veteran Jimmy Squibb won the first race under the new Provincial regime.

The story was very different where Cradley Heath was concerned. When the midlanders gathered in the pits before the start, there was no Ivor Brown, no Eric Hockaday and no John Hart.

The billing for the match was changed to Exeter versus a Cradley Heath Select, with the riders taking the place of the missing Cradley stars of considerable interest to those with an interest in the political implications of the encounter.

Two Poole riders, Ross Gilbertson and Tim Bungay, joined regular *Heathens* Harry Bastable, Derek Timms, Alan Totney and John Edwards in the Cradley Select side, suggesting that the Dorset side was unlikely to have many team problems caused by the illegal status.

The third substitute was Alby Golden, a National League rider with Southampton in 1963, slated by the Control Board to ride in the National League for Wimbledon or West Ham in 1964, but reported as having signed for Provincial League newcomers Newport and certainly present at the County Ground, riding 'black' and filling the final hole in the Cradley side.

The response of the National League promoters to the refusal of the Provincial League to allow one of its teams to be promoted was the re-opening of West Ham. Coventry's Ken McKinlay, pictured with team-mates Les Owen (left) and an injured Jim Lightfoot, was transferred to the East London side, which was controlled by the Coventry management team of Alan Sanderson and Charles Ochiltree. During the split Owen and Lightfoot remained loyal to Coventry and the National League.

The crowd saw Exeter win 45-33, but missed out on what would have been a second half treat. New Zealander Ivan Mauger, who had made a successful return to British speedway with Newcastle in 1963, was booked in at the County Ground for a series of second half match races, but in the event decided not to ride.

Mauger gained brownie points from the Exeter management by driving to Devon from his Manchester home to explain his reasons for not competing, rather than simply telephoning to cancel. Even at that stage the future six-times World Champion had ambitions for conquering the global stage, and was concerned that riding 'black' would harm his aspirations.

At the end of the meeting the Provincial promoters returned home convinced that things were going to work out for them, while the National League chiefs and the Control Board were able to claim that the absence of the three leading Cradley riders meant the match that had taken place had been a mere poor substitute for what had been advertised. The dilemma still obviously facing many riders, including an up-and-coming star like Mauger, must also have heartened the 'official' side.

The patchy response to the Provincial rebellion did not last for too long.

On the following Saturday, after yet more threats and more lobbying, the return leg of the challenge match took place in the Black Country. Ivor Brown, appointed Cradley captain, took his place in the side and scored a flawless maximum 12 points, and was joined by John Hart.

The third of the Cradley riders absent from the third leg, Eric Hockaday, was at least present at Dudley Wood, albeit as a spectator. Today he remembers:

> I was still holding back because I wanted to see what was going to happen. Then Ivor and John rode in the match, and Ivan Mauger and Clive Featherby rode in match races in the second half. After the meeting I took the plunge and signed my contract with Cradley.

Some of the promising stars of the Provincial League at first stayed legal and looked for hard-to-find opportunities at the National tracks, notably Colin Pratt. Without a PL track following the closure of Stoke at the end of 1963, Pratt was not keen on moving with one or two of his team mates to Reg Fearman's other interest at Long Eaton, and initially linked with National League Swindon. With few points being scored or money earned, and with a family to support, Pratt eventually switched back to the Provincial League, joining Hackney.

During the winter of 1963-64 the National League promoters, perhaps never wholly convinced that the raid on the Provincial League would succeed, decided to re-open West Ham, which Alan Sanderson had closed for speedway at the end of 1955.

The Sanderson/Ochiltree connection provided a ready-made heat leader for the re-

Bob Andrews' action in attempting to ride PL for Wolverhampton brought opposition from both Wimbledon and Wolves' riders. In happier times Andrews (right) is seen with Wimbledon team-mates Gerry Jackson (left) and Cyril Maidment. He eventually settled back into the Wimbledon team for the rest of 1964.

born *Hammers* in the shape of Ken McKinlay, transferred from Coventry, while the team was also boosted by three riders who in 1963 had performed in the Provincial League but who now decided for one reason or another to stay loyal to the National League.

Ray Cresp, who was to become an official of the Speedway Riders Association, had stepped down from the top tier to ride for PL St Austell, but did not hesitate to stick with the official set-up. He explained:

> The decision was not difficult at all, it seemed the right thing to do. I did not
> particularly like riding in the Provincial League, as I felt I just rode down to their level.

Although Colin Pratt eventually joined Hackney, the *Hawks* lost the services of two of their 1963 riders to West Ham. Norman Hunter proved one of the *Hammers'* successes in a tricky come-back season, and proved that it was possible to make the step up in status. Malcolm Simmons rode for Hackney in one PL meeting but after being banned and losing the right to compete in grass-track meetings, where as an up-and coming star he could earn good money, quickly returned to legitimacy with the *Hammers*.

The closure of Southampton at the end of '63 had freed up several riders. The new Provincial League promotion at Newport, initially a partnership between Mike Parker and the Foot family, was a natural home for three highly experienced former South-ampton men, one-time England test rider Dick Bradley, his team-mate Alby Golden, and Peter Vandenberg.

Although all three of these riders had been named in National League team line-ups for 1964, and were more than capable performers at the higher level, they had no qualms about a step down to the Provincial League.

Throughout the entire National League/Provincial League stand-off, Mike Parker's Wolverhampton remained at the eye of the storm. Wolverhampton, for a variety of reasons, experienced rider problems at the start of the campaign, and made a slow start to what the management had hoped would be a defence of the league title.

The season was well underway when the team which had refused to be coerced into accepting promotion appeared to have captured the signature on a 'pirate' contract of the highest-profile National League rider to decide to forsake legal racing for the PL. Heat leader Bob Andrews, a fixture at Plough Lane for the best part of a decade, appeared in Wolverhampton colours in the *Wolves'* 52-26 win over Sunderland on Friday May 22. He was one of several National League riders who saw the opportunity for more meetings

Perhaps the most bitter episode of the civil war occurred when Bob Andrews, an established National League rider with Wimbledon, signed for PL Wolverhampton, only to be served (pictured) with a High Court injunction while warming up his bike in the Hackney pits.

(and earnings) in the PL, and his experiences went on to form a significant test case.

The next evening, at Coventry, Andrews reported for duty with Wimbledon, visiting Brandon Stadium in a Britannia Shield fixture. He did not actually appear on the track that evening with, as *Speedway Star* reported, both teams objecting to riding either with or against Andrews who, after considerable pressure had been exerted, withdrew from the meeting.

On the same evening Coventry included Bryan Elliott, who in the same edition of the *Star* had been reported as having signed for Provincial League side Long Eaton.

Bob Andrews' second appearance for Wolverhampton was scheduled to be at Hackney. *Speedway Star* published a photograph showing an official of the High Court serving an injunction, obtained by *Dons* promoter Ronnie Greene, upon the rider whilst he warmed up his machine in the pits at Waterden Road.

Bob Andrews returned to action for Wimbledon the night after the Hackney incident, at Oxford and continued to ride for the *Dons* for the remainder of the season. Andrews still vividly recalls the incidents surrounding his attempted switch to the Provincial League:

> I was warming up my bike when an official-looking man in a smart suit asked above the roar of the machines if I was Bob Andrews. The Hackney promoter Len Silver phoned Mike Parker, who confirmed that there was an injunction to stop me riding.
>
> While waiting for the case to come to court, Ronnie Greene at Wimbledon had got the other *Dons* riders to agree not to ride with me. As some of the Wolverhampton team were not very happy about the situation either, I was stuck.
>
> I continued to turn up for Wimbledon meetings to at least show that I was honouring my contract with them. Eventually Greene had to persuade the Wimbledon riders to ride with me in the team. If he had not, the judge would have ruled that Wimbledon was effectively stopping me from earning a living.
>
> I was fined £100 by the Speedway Control Board (although it was never actually paid. It's fair to say it was the lowest point of my career. The good thing that came out of it was that my case brought the dispute between the two leagues to a head and probably helped to bring about the 1965 merger.

When the British League was eventually formed, Bob Andrews got his original wish and moved to Wolverhampton.

Wolverhampton eventually saw their 1964 team problems solved when PL newcomers Sunderland folded prematurely. *Wolves* obtained Australians Jim Airey and Gordon Guasco, and New Zealander Colin McKee, from the *Saints*.

With riders switching between the leagues, court injunctions and a welter of threats, accusations and counter-threats, the speedway media was never short of a news story in 1964. Yet for the majority of the fans, and perhaps surprisingly also the riders themselves, the dispute meant relatively little.

James Bond, a Birmingham fan from the late 1940s onwards, and later a cycle speedway rider, had nursed an ambition ride himself for many years. After National Service, during which he was a member of the Royal Signals display team, in 1963 he followed his former cycle speedway team-mate Dave Hemus to Monmore Green, Wolverhampton.

> I had a couple of successful second half rides at Wolverhampton and managed to break into the team. It was the final season at Monmore Green for Graham Warren, who had been my favourite rider at Birmingham from 1949 onwards, and you can imagine what it felt like riding in the same team as my hero.
>
> When it came to the start of the 1964 season and all the talk of a split, it was not an issue for me at all to sign a contract again for Wolverhampton in the Provincial League. I was just a wet-behind-the-ears first year rider. I would go anywhere for a ride and the politics were really of no interest to me.
>
> I did, like all the other PL riders, receive a letter from the Speedway Control Board saying that a special court had been held in London to consider my breaches of the rules on riding on authorised tracks. The letter said I had been found guilty (there was a capital G) and was suspended sine die.
>
> It really meant nothing to me and I just kept on riding like everyone else. The funny thing though is that although the Board was quick enough to send out a letter saying I was banned, they didn't write again when the suspensions were eventually lifted.
>
> Theoretically, I am probably still suspended!

One area in which the suspensions did have a genuine effect upon riders concerned other forms of motor cycle sport. Many riders also competed on grass tracks, including Bond's manager at Wolverhampton, Bill Bridgett, who was a major star in the sport. James Bond recalls:

> A lot of little grass track circuits opened up to give the Provincial League riders a chance to still compete, including a couple at Brownhills in Staffordshire, while I believe Glyn Chandler opened a track near Cirencester.

One trump card the National League had to play in 1964 was the first-ever test series between Great Britain and Russia, with matches in early July at Wembley, Coventry and Belle Vue (the latter providing a first-ever visit to Hyde Road for the author).

Great Britain, with Barry Briggs and Ray Cresp augmenting home riders including How, McKinlay, Nigel Boocock, and Mike Broadbank, proved much too strong for the Russians, winning 73-35 at Wembley, 56-52 at Coventry, and 71-37 at Belle Vue. There were nearly 27,000 spectators at the Empire Stadium, and packed stadia in the Midlands and Manchester too, and the series gave racing at the top level a huge boost.

The annual Whit Monday Internationale at Wimbledon was the third National League success, as 16,230 spectators saw Barry Briggs win the title and the £250 speedway machine which was the prize.

The success of the Russian test series and the continuing appeal of the Internationale was food for thought all round.

While all the inter-league shenanigans was taking place, Oxford (basement club in 1963) shocked the speedway world by winning what was to prove the last National League title of the era, helped by Gordon McGregor (pictured).

Despite the very considerable Provincial League success, there was a clear message that there was a strong continuing appetite for racing at the highest level, involving the very best riders from around the world.

It was perhaps the ultimate irony of the 1964 season that the final name on a National League trophy that over its decades of existence had been dominated by Wembley, Belle Vue and, latterly, Wimbledon, should be unfashionable Oxford.

Shrewd signings produced a *Cheetahs* team without a weak link. Danish star Arne Pander stayed clear of injury, Ron How was signed from Wimbledon and Oxford were propelled to the championship by the solid scoring of the track's G-force of Jack Geran, Colin Goody, Ronnie Genz and another new signing, Jimmy Gooch, who came in from Norwich. Eddie Reeves was one of the few young riders to make a success of deciding to stick with the National League in 1964 and with John Bishop he completed the picture of success for the *Cheetahs*.

Newcastle and Hackney disputed the Provincial League throughout the season, with the *Diamonds* having a three point advantage in the final table. The previous year's champions, Wolverhampton, did well to come through their early season rider problems to finish third.

Individually, Ivan Mauger dominated the season, averaging almost 12 points from his 34 official matches. He had a fine record in the Silver Sash match race championship and retained his Provincial League Riders Championship title in the controversial final at Belle Vue.

Second to Mauger in both the averages and in the PLRC was Charlie Monk, whose achievement in scoring more than 11 points match was a bright spot in a comeback season which saw Glasgow finish bottom of the table.

In many ways, despite the successes of Newcastle and Hackney – the latter club greatly boosted by Len Silver's switch from Exeter and the signing of Colin Pratt when he returned from his National League period – the Provincial League team of the year in 1964 was Newport. The enthusiasm of the fans matched that experienced by speedway in the immediate post-war era, with crowds of up to 10,000 at home and huge travelling contingents, including an estimated 1,000 fans who went to Cradley to see the *Wasps* win the PL knock-out cup.

The back-biting continued throughout the season, with both sides in the dispute claiming victories. There is little doubt that the National League and its RAC/ACU backers were astounded by the efficiency of the 'pirate' operation, particularly in finding competent referees and other officials to run the meetings.

One particular feather in the cap for the provincials came when one of the most respected men in the sport, Lt Col Vernon Brook, a former chairman of the Control

Board and very much seen as an establishment figure, threw in his lot with the Provincials. The Provincial Speedway League Promoters Association persuaded Lt Col Brook to chair its own appeals court, an essential part of being seen to run the sport in a fair manner.

A season that had begun with recriminations inevitably ended the same way.

The Provincial League Promoters Association had a contract with Belle Vue (Manchester) Ltd for the highlight of the PL season, the Riders Championship Final, to be staged at Hyde Road. Belle Vue was determined to honour the contract and the meeting took place.

The Control Board promptly suspended Belle Vue, and the *Aces* responded by riding challenge matches on PL tracks. The National League and the Control Board, still unsure of what was going to happen in 1965, quickly thought better of a move which could have driven one of the jewels in their crown into the hands of the opposition, and rescinded the ban.

By this stage of the season, although the enquiry demanded by the PL promoters and eventually conceded by the RAC and the ACU was still in the future, there is ample reason to believe that the National League rump, despite the success of West Ham and the viability of the 1964 senior competition, were ready to accept that the prevailing state of affairs simply could not continue.

The sale of the Norwich stadium rumoured earlier, became a sad reality, meaning there were just six assured National League starters for 1965. It is at least possible that Charles Ochiltree could have persuaded his fellow NL promoters to repeat the 1964 West Ham experience and re-open Blackbird Road, Leicester, still part of the Midland Sports Stadiums combine.

The RAC, at the request of the Provincial League promoters, at last took positive action, appointing the eminent lawyer Lord Shawcross, Attorney General in the 1945-51 Labour government, to head an enquiry into the governance of the sport.

Was this the determining factor in brokering a peace deal between the National League and the Provincial League, or had some sort of merger between the warring factions become inevitable before Lord Shawcross and his assessors from the Royal Automobile Club had even begun their examination of how speedway racing in Britain was operated.

Rick France had been a member of Wolverhampton's Provincial League championship side in 1963. He was, however, only on loan from Charles Ochiltree's Coventry National League side, and when the split occurred he stayed loyal to his parent club.

One formerly prominent Provincial League rider who stayed clear of the civil war was Tony Robinson. He had retired to concentrate on his haulage business and resisted attempts to get him to return to the saddle, as evidenced by these telegrams from promoters eager for his services.

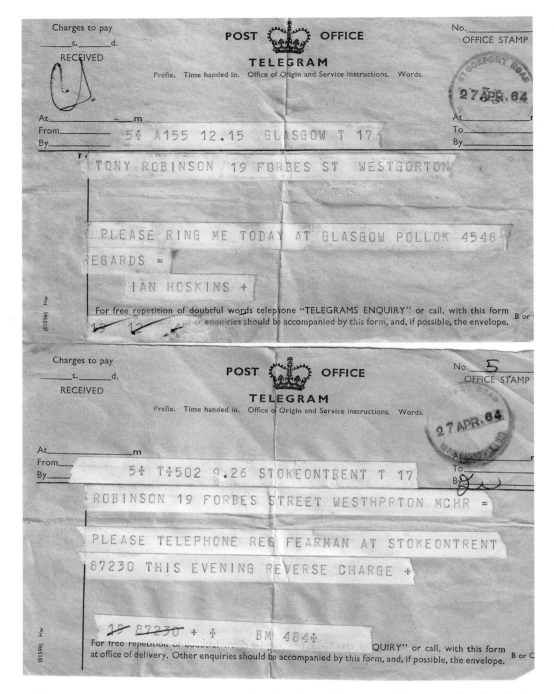

By the late autumn of 1964 it is a fair bet that the National League chiefs, which effectively meant Ochiltree and Greene of Wimbledon, realised the game was up and that there was no way the Provincial League could be cowed into submission.

In that sense, it could be argued that the much-vaunted Shawcross Inquiry, served only to reveal the obvious, that the National League promoters were seriously out of line legally in attempting to coerce the Provincial League. In the end, the Shawcross proposals may well only have crossed the Ts and dotted the Is of an inevitable merger, or what could perhaps more realistically be described as a swallowing of the rump of the Nationals by the triumphant Provincials.

Chapter eleven

ONE BIG LEAGUE
United for a bright future

I T WAS the Christmas present every speedway fan in Britain had put in pole position when they compiled their wish lists in the late autumn of 1964.

A fortnight or so before the big day, when they opened their copies of *Speedway Star*, there before their eyes on the magazine's first news page was the banner headline announcing, in capital letters and in a type-size double anything usually seen in the publication, ONE BIG LEAGUE.

The long and bitter dispute between the National League and the Provincial League was over. As the *Star* said: "It's over bar the shouting. One big league. Eighteen tracks. Suspensions lifted. There in a nutshell is the speedway format for 1965."

The story below the heading occupied almost all of the rest of the page. It covered not only the bullet points referred to in the introduction, but also gave readers some insight into the thinking on such important topics as the future of the Control Board, almost universally felt to be an ineffective body as it had been constituted to that point, foreign riders, and, crucially, what effect the proposed new structure was likely to have on the ordinary speedway supporter.

What the article singularly, and amazingly, failed to do was to tell the reader the story behind the story. The second paragraph of the article announced that the RAC probe headed by Lord Shawcross had met on December 3 and subsequently announced its findings, having heard recommendations from promoters from both the National and Provincial Leagues. Perhaps justifiably, given the season of the year and the spirit of peace and goodwill apparently breaking out across the speedway boundaries, the reporting concentrated on the recommendation and what it meant for speedway in the immediate, and hopefully in the long-term, future.

What it did not tell the reader in any detail whatsoever was just exactly what the Shawcross Inquiry findings had actually amounted to. A new control board, more say for all of the game's promoters, rather than a handful of bigwigs, one big league, the lifting of the 'blacking' of Provincial League riders, the issue of levelling team strengths and new regulations for foreign riders were essentially the *consequences* of the Shawcross Inquiry, and were obviously of prime importance.

For those interested in the way speedway governed itself, and curious about the real reasons which had caused the 1964 split, it would have useful to have known what Shawcross discovered about the state of the sport's administration. For given the shake-up he recommended, it is hardly likely that he was much impressed.

Anyone who has been grilled by any form of official hearing, whether it be a House of Commons Select Committee or an internal inquiry into failings in a private company or public body, will have experienced a certain number of qualms at the prospect.

Those called upon to give evidence to the Shawcross Inquiry, whether they were from the RAC, ACU, Control Board, National League or Provincial League, must have been somewhat awestruck by the stature of the man who was to delve into the organisation of speedway racing in Great Britain.

Hartley William Shawcross was Attorney General in the Attlee Labour government of 1945 to 1951. Knighted in 1945, he was Chief Prosecutor for the United Kingdom at the Nuremburg war trials, facing Nazi leaders such as Goering, Himmler, Hess and their like across the bar of the courtroom, and helping to send many of them to the gallows.

It looked a bit like a sledgehammer to crack a nut in the context of the dispute between speedway's warring leagues, but the Royal Automobile Club in 1964 was the most influential body in motor sport, and lawyers, no matter what their stature, are for hire.

Shawcross had form as far as speedway was concerned. Despite winning the initial Division Three title in 1947, Eastbourne struggled to attract crowds to their track some miles out of the resort in the Sussex countryside, in the days before much private car ownership.

Promoter Charles Dugard moved the team down the coast to Hasting, where the local football club's Pilot Field ground could be adapted for speedway. Hastings' *Saxons* were much more successful in attracting spectators, but aroused the ire of local residents.

After two seasons of racing a High Court injunction was obtained banning speedway from the Pilot Field. The name of the high profile lawyer briefed by the local residents

Peace has returned to speedway, the British league has been formed to replace the National and Provincial leagues, and the British League Promoters Association formed to effectively run the sport under the aegis of a reformed and less powerful Control Board. Some of the main protagonists in the 'civil war' are pictured here, including Charles Ochiltree of Coventry (back row, far left), Ronnie Greene of Wimbledon (front row, far right), and Mike Parker (Wolverhampton and Newcastle), second from right at the front, next to his old adversary Greene.

to argue their case was none other than the current Attorney General, Sir Hartley Shawcross.

It is intriguing that the issue on which the Shawcross Inquiry turned was apparently one which had been central to the status of speedway since its inception in the UK. It was the 'sport or entertainment' argument all over again.

The dividing line between sport in its purest sense and the world of business in a market society remains a tricky one. Governing bodies in sport have widespread powers which, if implemented to the full, can have a major effect on the financial well-being and even the future survival of a member club.

If a professional football club, unable to pay its debts, goes into administration, the governing body can deduct points, a punishment that is often sufficient to mean relegation for the club, and a consequent reduction not only in status but often in income.

The crucial issue that Lord Shawcross, in essence, was being asked to rule upon in the late autumn of 1964 concerned the precise status of a speedway team.

Was this status similar to that of a football club which, although generally fully professional and usually a limited company, was (at that period in history at least) essentially not an organisation primarily designed to personally benefit its shareholders or outright proprietor?

A professional football club in principle sought to produce a surplus of income and expenditure primarily to re-invest in its playing staff and facilities.

Speedway teams, the argument went, had an entirely different status. The rights to promote the sport at a specific venue were owned by an individual or a company, and the profits generated from the speedway were primarily for the benefit of that individual or company.

Former National Leaguers Coventry won the very first British League match, beating ex-Provincial League Cradley Heath. The very first race win was taken by *Bees'* Nigel Boocock (pictured in England colours) over top PL man Ivor Brown of Cradley.

As such, speedway promotions were businesses in the true sense of the term, and for a body such as the Control Board, backed by the RAC and the ACU, to attempt to order a promoter to behave in a way that he believed could prejudice the success of his business was, in effect, a restraint of trade.

Mike Parker at Wolverhampton, carrying on a successful business in the form of promoting a Provincial League speedway team, attracting good-sized crowds at a level of the sport which had much lower overheads, particularly in terms of payments to riders, than the National League, was being ordered to make a step up to a higher league with higher expenses, but little likelihood of larger attendances.

Parker and Wolverhampton, as the 1963 Provincial League champions, represented the team most in line for a forced elevation to the National League, and as such serves as the most suitable illustration, although there is plenty of evidence that the desperate senior promoters approached other managements in the lower tier, as they attempted to keep their franchise alive.

In the end, the evidence suggests that Lord Shawcross decided that speedway was primarily entertainment, and its individual tracks were businesses. The Control Board had no right to order an individual business to take a step that might prove harmful to its current and future profitability or its very existence.

The Shawcross ruling meant the end for both the Control Board in its existing form and for the National League. As suggested in the previous chapter, it is highly likely that Charles Ochiltree and Ronnie Greene in particular had already come to the conclusion that the status quo and their jealously-guarded privileges, such as the right to the major portion of World Final income, were becoming increasingly untenable.

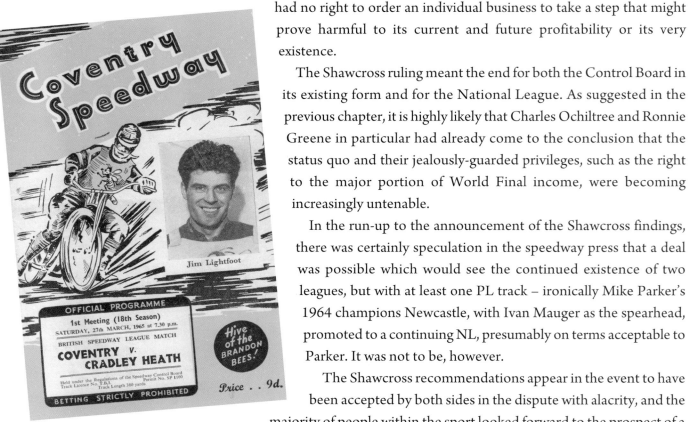

Jim Lightfoot

In the run-up to the announcement of the Shawcross findings, there was certainly speculation in the speedway press that a deal was possible which would see the continued existence of two leagues, but with at least one PL track – ironically Mike Parker's 1964 champions Newcastle, with Ivan Mauger as the spearhead, promoted to a continuing NL, presumably on terms acceptable to Parker. It was not to be, however.

The Shawcross recommendations appear in the event to have been accepted by both sides in the dispute with alacrity, and the majority of people within the sport looked forward to the prospect of a single league. As Ian Hoskins said:

The programme cover for the historic first British League match at Brandon Stadium, Coventry in 1965.

> Sanity at last prevailed. Ronnie Greene and Charles Ochiltree were resigned to having to eat at the same table as their former country cousins and the sport then got down to a complete revolution that was to be the salvation of speedway for years to come.

The merger of the rump of the National League with the Provincial League to form a single British League with 18 teams meant the highest number of teams in one division in the sport's history, if you discount, as you surely must, the unwieldy and chaotic English League of 1928.

A new Control Board, ceding much of its authority to a new British Speedway Promoters Association, was appointed, and planning went ahead for what promised to be an exciting 1965 campaign. Although the settlement between speedway's warring parties received a widespread welcome, not everyone was feeling totally positive as the 1965 season got underway.

Many ordinary National League fans appeared to appreciate the exclusivity and elite nature of the competition. They were seeing the cream of the world's riders in action, including Swedish and, on a more restricted basis, Polish stars and the fact that it was essentially the same familiar faces appearing on their circuits from week to week did not appear to be a major issue.

Fans at former Provincial League matches saw all the former National League stars in 1965, including Nigel Boocock of Coventry (left) and Oxford's spectacular Danish rider Arne Pander (right).

Some were quite vocal about their opposition to the formation of one big league. Mrs Dorothy Charles-Batson was a name to be conjured with at Wimbledon. A fortnight after the announcement of the peaceful settlement of the inter-league dispute, she wrote in scathing terms to the *Speedway Star*. Showing less concern for the adage of goodwill to all men than most people in the sport at this time (the edition of the magazine in which her letter was published was dated 25 December) she wrote:

> One big league for speedway! So we shall now only see each team once during the season. A lot of teams far from National League standard which will sicken NL supporters.
>
> At Wimbledon last season (1964), although we didn't win many races or matches, we had the finest meetings there for many a year. Every meeting was a real humdinger, who can possibly deny that.

Riders like multi-World Champion Barry Briggs were a big draw at tracks like Long Eaton in Derbyshire, which had never seem top-level racing before. Here Briggs (right), riding for Swindon, is headed by rising home star Ray Wilson.

The thought of what we shall get in 1965 with all the mediocre Provincial riders, bar a very, very few, leaves my heart like lead and my hopes of a speedway boom very much dashed. No top foreigners. No gate draws. That's for sure.

The letter was an outdated echo of attitudes in both the pre-war and post-war eras, when fans at the London circuits had consistently criticised the provincial teams, with the exception to some extent of Belle Vue, regarding them as inferior to the capital-based sides.

Mrs Charles-Batson clearly had little confidence in the ability of the new administrative order in speedway to produce a league with sufficiently balanced teams to please the discerning palates of the National League faithful. The early weeks of the 1965 season produced evidence to both support and refute her view.

The initial handiwork of those charged with balancing team strengths produced some undoubtedly lop-sided line-ups. The former National League teams had for the most part retained their top riders but had seen much of the solid middle section of their teams transferred elsewhere. The benefits of the reallocation system to the ex-Provincial League outfits can best be described as patchy.

The historic first-ever British League match, at Brandon Stadium, Coventry, on Saturday 27 March 1965, provided an ideal case study of what had happened.

The *Bees'* team on that early spring evening, when compared to the side that rode its final National League match at Belle Vue in October 1964, had retained top man Nigel Boocock and the long-serving Ron Mountford and Jim Lightfoot, both generally considered heat-leader standard, when at their best, at the top level. Also there for the *Bees* were two men regarded as up and coming, in the shape of Rick France and Col Cottrell.

Out of a *Bees* team which had finished third in the seven-team 1964 National League had gone a star man in the form of Ken McKinlay, transferred to West Ham, one-time Australian Test star Jack Biggs, effectively a Brandon reserve in 1964, and reliable local boy Les Owen. The team was made up, and this is where the lop-sided effect really cut in, of two Coventry second-half riders with precious little experience of league racing at any level, Howie Booton and Fred Hodder. Owen refused to ride elsewhere and was eventually reinstated.

Cradley, rock bottom of the Provincial League in 1964, tracked a side identical to the team which wore the green and white colours of the *Heathens* at the end of that season. So much for balancing the strengths of the teams in the new big league.

Cradley's top man, and one of the undoubted stars of the Provincial League, Ivor Brown might have led Coventry's Boocock into the first bend of the first-ever British league heat, but he had to be satisfied with second place when the riders crossed the finishing line.

The *Heathens* too had to be content with second best, with many commentators rating their 47-31 defeat as a fair performance in the circumstances.

The fact that Coventry had retained the core of their side from the National League, compared to Cradley's absolute lack of strengthening, was to be reflected at the end of the season. The *Bees* finished in a gratifying third place in the new league; Cradley were third from bottom, behind two other woefully weak former Provincial outfits, Edinburgh and Long Eaton.

England stars old and new. Ray Wilson, who went on to captain an England Speedway World Cup winning side and earn the nickname 'World Cup Willie' won a Silver Sash Match Race round at Belle Vue and is publicly congratulated by *Aces* manager Dent Oliver, a former England star himself.

After the long season had finished, it was perhaps no great surprise that the two sides above Coventry at the top of the table, champions West Ham and runners-up Wimbledon, together with fourth-placed side Oxford, were all ex-National Leaguers.

Rather more surprising was the fact that the two other former National League sides, Belle Vue and Swindon, finished in 14th and 15th spots respectively, just above the ex-Provincial League basement boys from the Black Country, Scotland's capital city, and Derbyshire.

Predictably, the welcome for the first British League in 1965 from the sport's main media was also cautious. Whilst welcoming the restoration of peace, the *Speedway Star* wondered if an 18-team league would prove too unwieldy, and also worried about the effect of losing some of the top overseas performers.

Former Provincial League tracks also began to see international competition at the highest level. Polish club side Gornik Rybnik toured in 1965 and here Eric Hockaday of Cradley gives a lift to Gornik's Joachim Maj.

Initially, when peace was declared and the National League formed, it was intended that only overseas riders prepared to live in Britain, at least during the speedway season, would be eligible to ride for British League sides. Given the drawing power of the Swedes in particular, the policy was not long-lived.

Looking back with hindsight, over a span of not far short of five decades, the British League **was**, problems of rider allocation and other issues notwithstanding, a major success story.

The first boom in speedway was to a considerable degree a welcome for an exciting novelty. The post-war golden age owed much to a reaction to a new-found freedom after six years of a highly restricted lifestyle. It has been said that in the late 1940s, the

The British League went to considerable (if not always altogether successful) lengths to equalise team strengths as much as possible. Cradley fans were not too happy when the high-scoring John Hart (left) and Eric Hockaday were transferred to Sheffield *Tigers*.

public was so starved of entertainment that two men playing marbles in the street would quickly draw a crowd.

While the Provincial League in 1960 saved speedway from complete marginalisation and paved the way for the events in 1965, it had a considerable turnover of member tracks. The British League achieved both outstanding success and, for a remarkable 30 years gave the sport a stability and a prolonged period of prosperity that it had never previously experienced, attracting many, many new spectators, at a time when the swinging sixties offered a great variety of other attractions.

To make speedway cool – and it undoubtedly was to a large degree – in such a feverish climate of changing and more liberal lifestyles was a massive achievement and the promoters who brought about the success of the new competition deserve great praise.

New stars emerged alongside the older favourites as the British League began to prove a big success. Belle Vue introduced Swedish discovery Soren Sjosten (right) , pictured warming up his machine in the West Ham pits alongside long-established Ace Dick Fisher.

There was plenty of in-fighting within the new British Speedway Promoters Association to be sure – it would not have been speedway without it – but to their credit, the old guard of Greene and Ochiltree did what was necessary to work with the upstarts from the Provincial League.

The British League survived from 1965 to 1995. It maintained a membership of between 16 and 19 clubs until the boom period began to subside in the early eighties, running alongside a second tier of speedway which operated under several different names, including, rather confusingly, a return to the National League title for what was effectively a second division.

By the time the British League was re-named as the Premier League in 1995, it had chalked up 30 years of existence. In terms of years, that was a little less than the original National League's run from 1932 to 1964, but that competition was suspended from 1940 to 1946.

British League action intensified the rivalry between Black Country sides Wolverhampton and Cradley Heath. *Wolves'* Australian star Jim Airey leads out of the fourth bend at Monmore Green, from l-r Eric Hockaday (Cradley), Cyril Francis (*Wolves*) and, unusually in last place, Ivor Brown of Cradley, with a white jersey under his race jacket.

A Wolverhampton British League side, l-r Alan Cowland, James Bond, Peter Vandenberg, Gordon Guasco (later to lose his life in a track accident), Brian Maxted, Cyril Francis and co-promoter Bill Bridgett. On the machine is skipper Peter Jarman.

The British League brought remarkable prosperity and stability to speedway for many years. The Long Eaton promotion had struggled with only moderate crowds and difficulties with maintaining the track, used for frequent stock car racing. The licence was transferred to Leicester and the new *Lions* team attracted large crowds. Pictured are former Long Eaton man Norman Storer (left) and his new team-mate John Hart.

Whether the late 1964 peace deal was truly brokered by Lord Shawcross and the RAC, or whether the National League promoters had already seen the light and realised that a merger was the only way forward, the British League that resulted not only brought speedway a new era of prosperity, and respect, but also made possible the sport's survival into a new century.

More action from Monmore Green, Wolverhampton. James Bond (left) leads the way from *Wolves* team-mate Tommy Sweetman (centre) and Sverre Harrfeldt of West Ham.

Although riders not domiciled in the UK were initially banned from the new British League, a new wave of riders from Sweden and elsewhere soon became familiar to British fans. Future World Champion Anders Michanek of Sweden attempts to straighten out his forks after sliding gently to grief.

EPILOGUE
Thrills, spills and a roll of honour

Long before health and safety became an inescapable part of everyday life, a paragraph printed as a mandatory section of all official match programmes spelled out the uncompromising message that 'speedway is dangerous.' Despite uninformed claims to the contrary, the sport is not only dangerous but often deadly, as the roll of honour of some 250 riders killed around the world in track incidents amply testifies. The real dangers inherent in speedway lead in most cases to a very real camaraderie among the riders. Frequent reunions, many organised by the veterans' organisation, the World Speedway Riders Association, are well attended and old friendships are revived and track rivalries recalled.

THE AUSTRALIAN pioneer Wilfred Spencer Lamont, better known to the dirt track world as 'Cyclone Billy' Lamont, was billed as the man with a month to live, a reference to his spectacular, no-holds barred, safety-fence-scraping style of riding.

The fact that the ploy worked for somewhat longer than a month after Lamont should logically have met his end, proved that the early speedway promoters had the knack of being able to fool at least a portion of the public for quite a lot of the time.

Lamont's name has survived in the collective speedway memory down to the present day, much more for his reputation for breath-taking recklessness than for actual track success. You will search in vain for his name in the lists of those who won

That sinking feeling ... Happily, as is the case in a great many speedway crashes, both riders walked away with nothing more than bruising.

Tom Farndon's death in 1935 caused great mourning among New Cross supporters.

England star Frank Charles died not in a speedway accident but in a glider crash in the Derbyshire Peak District in 1939.

championships, although he did ride for some time at the top level, for Wimbledon and Wembley, and gained a handful of Australian test caps.

Cyclone Billy's style and reputation no doubt earned him plenty of hard cash in terms of appearance money, to make up for the lack of trophies in his sideboard. The same promoters who exploited the potential dangers of his technique would willingly pay extra for the type of rider who drew a crowd.

Yet far from making an early entry into speedway Valhalla in a blaze of glory, Lamont survived his notoriety in the sport's wild and woolly pioneering era of the late 1920s and early 1930s to become a popular journeyman rider in the much more sober latter years of the '30s, representing a number of lower division provincial clubs, including Plymouth, Nottingham, Sheffield, and Newcastle, now as a (relatively) steady, middle-range points scorer.

Harold Lander, who went on to work in the film industry in Australia after World War Two, had as a boy watched Lamont at Nottingham White City in 1937 and had been thrilled by the Australian.

> By the time I saw him regularly he wasn't winning many races but he was exciting to watch. Billy never changed from leg-trailing to the new foot-forward style of racing. I stood near the bend and had to duck when he came round to avoid being covered in cinders.

After Lander had moved to Australia and into the film industry he conceived the idea of making a film about the early years of speedway and tracked down Billy Lamont, who was working as a night watchman in a factory. Lamont had lost touch with speedway and admitted he hadn't even looked at his press cuttings for many years.

The hype surrounding Billy Lamont provides an excellent illustration of speedway's often uneasy relationship with its darker side.

Depending upon your viewpoint, the blatant suggestion that one set of spectators would have a grandstand seat for the inevitable demise of a daredevil rider can seem ghoulish and in bad taste, while the more discerning, even at the time, no doubt saw it as a transparently ridiculous attempt to tempt through the turnstiles those for whom the racing itself was not enough of a draw card.

Silly as 'the man with a month to live' tag may seem today, the suggestion it carried of the perils of the dirt track has to a large degree been justified by the number of fatalities recorded across the history of speedway.

The modern-day equivalent of the publicity surrounding Lamont's on-the-edge riding style must be the commercially-produced DVD montages of crashes that can be bought for a few pounds, whilst television trailers for speedway often include some of the more spectacular pile-ups, captured much more graphically than in the past given the superior camerawork of the twenty-first century.

Broadsiding a 500cc motor cycle, with faster acceleration than a Formula One racing car, around a short circuit, without the benefit of brakes, and coming within an inch or so of another competitor's machine or body at speeds of more than 60 miles per hour on the straights, IS potentially highly dangerous, and requires not only courage and skill but also excellent judgment.

The motorcycle sports claimed as predecessors to speedway racing, the American board and flat track racing, claimed several victims in the years before World War One. The first recorded fatality in speedway in its Australian form appears to be H J Stockdale, who died as a result of a crash at Penrith, New South Wales, in March 1925.

England's first recorded track deaths occurred at Stamford Bridge, where

The white-leathered Australian star Ken Le Breton, killed in a test match crash in Sydney, described in this chapter by eye-witness Reg Fearman, who was a member of the opposing England team.

Charlie Biddle died in May 1928, and at Cleveland Park, Middlesbrough a year later, where the sport claimed the life of Dennis Atkinson.

Fatal speedway crashes have over the years occurred for a variety of reasons, with several contributing factors. In earlier times the standard of safety helmets and the riders' leather protective clothing was of variable quality and modern-day items such as back protectors were unknown.

In the search for any sort of pattern for fatalities and accidents leading to serious and paralysing injury, it quickly becomes clear that neither age or experience makes much difference when circumstances combine to create a fatal speedway accident.

Riders can part company with their machines for a variety of reasons, with both mechanical and human failings to blame. Riders can hit a loose lump of shale or a particularly slick section of the track surface and be thrown off balance. Wheels can lock, engines can seize, and mechanical parts can work loose.

The injury that effectively ended the promising Division One career of Birmingham's Geoff Bennett came about when the front wheel of the rider in front of him literally dropped out of its forks. Bennett laid down his machine but could not avoid hitting the fallen rider and he suffered a compound fracture of his right leg.

Riders have died in their first race in front of a paying crowd, or even before getting to that stage, losing control of their machines during private practice sessions at training tracks. On occasions fate appeared to have handed novices struggling to make a breakthough in the sport a long-awaited chance to make their name.

New Zealander John Garmston came to the UK in 1931 and linked up with Nottingham, then competing in the Southern League, along with speedway's giants such as Wembley and Belle Vue. The standard of racing was high, and Garmston had to be content with second half rides.

When a combination of poor results, falling crowds and a rider famine caused by injury led the Nottingham management to resign from the league mid season, the supporters raised the funds to stage a further meeting. Garmston, and other fringe riders, got their big chance, in an individual meeting.

For the New Zealander, it was his first – and last – competitive ride in Britain. During the race his front wheel came into contact with the rear wheel of the man in front – another common cause of a speedway crash.

Not all of the novices on the sport's roll of honour, cut down when receiving what appeared to be a big personal break, were youngsters with little or no experience of handling a racing motorcycle. Dick Jenkins, who received fatal injuries in his first appearance before a paying crowd at Plymouth in May 1951, was a 36-year-old father of two, who had been an active grass-track racer.

According to contemporary accounts Jenkins was 'thrilled' when offered a ride in a supplementary heat put on by the track management to give a trial to four novice riders. Coming out of the second bend he was seen to be having some difficulty controlling the machine but nevertheless rode down the back straight at Pennycross Stadium at what appeared to be full throttle. Appearing unable to negotiate the next bend, he literally rode up the safety fence and over the top.

At the other end of the scale the sport has throughout its history claimed the lives not just of aspirational novices, but also of genuine stars. The most high profile casualty in the 1930s was undoubtedly Tom Farndon, an idol of the fanatical supporters at New Cross in South London, many of whom, particularly the female fans, reacted to his death in a manner not unlike the scenes of mourning linked to the demise of screen idol Rudolf Valentino some years before.

Farndon was also young (24), highly successful, and cut off in his prime. It has been suggested on his behalf in recent years that he was the greatest speedway rider ever. The honours he had won during a fairly brief career – winning the Star Riders Championship, effectively the equivalent of the later World Championship, and the British Match Race Championship and the London Riders Championship in both 1934 and 1935 – provide strong supporting evidence for what can only be a highly subjective claim, given that his career was essentially a work in progress.

Born in Coventry, where his grave is still a place of pilgrimage for speedway fans, he started his racing career in the midlands city and later raced for Crystal Palace before transferring with that team to New Cross.

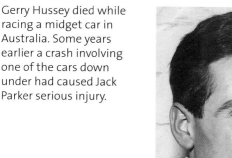

Gerry Hussey died while racing a midget car in Australia. Some years earlier a crash involving one of the cars down under had caused Jack Parker serious injury.

Ironically, given his success in major meetings, Farndon died after a collision with team-mate Ron Johnson in a low-key second half scratch race at the Old Kent Road track, being thrown from his machine and landing on his head. He died two days later without regaining consciousness. Thousands lined the streets to see his funeral.

In the early post-war era, one of speedway's real veterans, Joe Abbott, one of the sport's toughest men, fell victim to a track crash. The promotorial spin doctors of the late 1920s may have marketed Billy Lamont as a rider living on the brink of disaster, but in truth Abbott, in his late 40s and

perhaps postponing the inevitable end of a long career, had teetered on the precipice of disaster for some time.

Joe was one of speedway's northern pioneers, starting out with his local track in Burnley in 1929, before switching to Preston, Burnley's bitter Lancashire rivals in footballing terms, for two seasons. When the sport contracted in the north, he was good enough to find a place at the arch survivors, Belle Vue and stayed at the Hyde Road track until the outbreak of World War Two.

A pre-war England international, his partner in the *Aces* side was often Frank Charles, who had died while competing in a gliding competition in the Derbyshire Peak District in 1939.

Derek 'Tink' Maynard, an up-and-coming young Belle Vue rider, died in a crash with team-mate Maurice 'Slant' Paying at Norwich.

Abbott, already 37 years old when World War Two began, was one of the riders who competed throughout the hostilities at Belle Vue. He was surprisingly absent when fully competitive speedway resumed but returned to the scene in 1947, riding for Harringay Racers, a team which had also missed out on 1946.

He returned to the north for 1948, to ride for Bradford Boomerangs. Always prone to spectacular track crashes – his ability to bounce back time and time again earned him the additional nickname of the india rubber man – he used up another of his lives at West Ham in June 1949, in an early televised meeting.

On this occasion he was quite severely injured, but the swift intervention of ambulancemen proved to be a life-saver. Just over a year later, his luck ran out. Riding at Bradford's Odsal Stadium, again against West Ham, he fell in his second race, was struck by a following rider, and died instantly.

The riders decided to carry on with the meeting, although the crowd left the stadium unaware that the 48-year-old Abbott was dead. Ironically, he had recently been quoted as saying that he felt on top form, and hoped to race until he was 60.

The manner of Abbott's death was – and is – perhaps the source of a speedway rider's greatest fear. Competitors have accepted the hazards of the track for more than 80 years. Even the bravest will readily admit to dreading the circumstance where a rider in front of him falls, leaving those following behind just split seconds in which to take avoiding action.

One of the first things a speedway novice is taught is how to 'lay down' his machine – effectively voluntarily dropping it to the track surface – in the event of a rider falling in front of him. The danger in these encounters is not just with the rider who falls

Tony Robinson, at the time on the fringe of the Belle Vue team, was lodging with Tink Maynard and Tink's mother at the time of the fatal crash, and relates in this chapter how he learnt of the death of his team-mate and friend and was consoled by Peter Craven, who went to Maynard's Stockport home after riding in the match at Norwich.

originally, as is illustrated by the Geoff Bennett incident mentioned earlier, but undoubtedly swift action by following riders has saved many lives over the years.

Another high profile death in the early post-war period was that of Ken Le Breton, an Australian rider who had grabbed attention in his early days in Britain through his use of the then highly-unusual white racing leathers.

Le Breton's death, which occurred during an Australia–England test match in Sydney in January 1951, was one of those thankfully rare instances in speedway where the conspiracy theorists had a field day speculating on whether or not the incident was a pure accident.

Anyone who has played any kind of contact sport will on occasions have vowed retaliation at the earliest possible opportunity for some physical slight. Leaving the boot in place during the follow-up to a tackle in football, looking to intimidate with fast bowling to the body in cricket, and any one of a dozen imaginable kicks, gouges, punches or worse in rugby prompt the victim to say, 'I'll get him next time'.

In contact sports, foul play can lead to an injury serious enough to force a professional player out of his particular game, losing his livelihood. In recent times incidents have resulted in courtroom claims for compensation against another performer, or even prosecutions for assault. In speedway, the closest any form of motorised sport comes to

one-to-one physical contact, the end result of anything untoward could be instant death, or paralysis.

Le Breton died following a crash on the last bend of the last heat of the test match, on the narrow, banked track, more than 500 yards in length, at the Sydney Sports Ground, with a safety barrier consisting of a solid wall of concrete.

Attempting to pass England's Eddie Rigg on the last bend, Le Breton was, as a non-committal police statement would say after a road accident, 'in collision' with Rigg. His machine locked and he ran hard and direct into the fearsome safety barrier, dying the next day due to severe head injuries, including a fractured skull and a punctured lung.

What actually transpired that day in Sydney has been the subject of much controversy over the intervening years. In the first test match of the series, also at Sydney Showground, it is claimed that Le Breton bored under Rigg and rubbed his front wheel against his opponents left leg, a fairly common racing ploy designed to make a rider move out of the way.

The youngest member of the England team in the pits that night was Reg Fearman, later a leading speedway promoter, administrator and *Lions* team manager in an Australian series. He was on the spot when Rigg, angered by Le Breton's action, returned to the pits and spat out the words, 'I'll have the bastard.' Reg Fearman says today:

> Feuds and even vendettas did take place between riders, particularly in the
> 1940s and 1950s. Rigg's words are comments that hundreds of speedway riders
> have uttered.
>
> I can accept the description of the collision which states that Le Breton hit
> Rigg's rear wheel, possibly going for a gap that suddenly closed? All riders have
> sought to close a gap or have ridden another rider out wide to protect their own
> position, but I'm sure no one has ever done so with intent to maim another
> rider.
>
> If Eddie Rigg did close the gap or pull down on le Breton, it was certainly with
> no intent of such a drastic end result.

Peter Craven's own death, in a track crash during an end-of-season challenge match between Belle Vue and Edinburgh, at the Scottish capital's Old Meadowbank track in 1963, is still mourned by speedway fans throughout the world.

Louis Lawson of Belle Vue survived a fractured skull after crashing at the end of the 1953 season, ironically in a tussle with later fatal casualty Gerry Hussey. The incident ended Lawson's career and later in life he suffered a brain haemorrhage (also survived) which may have been connected to the crash.

The unfortunate John Garmston and Dick Jenkins dreamt of becoming top speedway riders, an ambition they were never to fulfil. Tom Farndon can safely be described as a superstar of speedway, before the term was in general usage. The veteran Joe Abbott and the still on-the-up Ken Le Breton were international riders of ability and determination.

Speedway has also claimed the lives of what can be fairly described as the solid club men, who had progressed through the novice ranks into a place in the starting line-up at the highest level of competition. Some of those in this category who subsequently died on the track may well have gone on to develop into stars, while others would simply have been content to enjoy their speedway in the second string positions in their teams.

Belle Vue has always had a strong reputation for developing talent. Despite speedway in the late 1950s being reduced to a single professional league, there were opportunities for riders with sufficient skills and determination to make their way in the sport.

In the summer of 1960, those opportunities were greatly increased with the creation of the Provincial League. So it was that on Saturday May 23 1960, two young riders nurtured at Belle Vue set off in different directions from a modest house in Stockport, to earn their living riding speedway.

Derek Maynard, known to everyone as 'Tink', lived with his widowed mother at the Stockport address. Lodging with them was a promising junior called Tony Robinson. With his mother away visiting relatives in her native north east of England, Maynard roused himself early and set off on the long journey south and east, along roads which even in the motorway era can be difficult, to ride for Belle Vue in the semi-final of the National Trophy at The Firs Stadium, Norwich.

Tony Robinson had a much shorter journey in prospect, south to the Sun Street Stadium at Hanley, Stoke-on-Trent, where he was riding for Sheffield, on loan from parent club Belle Vue.

At Norwich that evening the *Stars* team was a talented mix of experience and youth, with Australian veteran Aub Lawson, World Champion Ove Fundin, former cycle speedway ace and one-time teenage prodigy Billy Bales, former Wimbledon man Reg Trott and Japanese POW camp survivor Harry Edwards, a former Belle Vue rider.

The *Aces* tracked their own World Champion in the form of Peter Craven and had two New Zealanders in Ron Johnston and Bob Duckworth and an up-and-coming Swede, Gote Nordin.

The Firs, like Hyde Road in Manchester, was a big circuit, with no greyhound track, allowing the fans to get up close to the boarded safety fence to enjoy the racing which, in the case of a National Trophy match, was over 18 heats. Just a week earlier, in the first match of a two-legged tie, Belle Vue had won 66-42, with Norwich being kept in the race mainly by 17 points from six rides from Ove Fundin.

The first two heats of the match were drawn 3-3, maintaining Belle Vue's differential, and Norwich fans' hearts sank a little in the third race when Ron Johnston and Peter Craven recorded a 5-1 heat win. The tide then started to turn in the Norwich direction, as Harry Edwards and local boy Derek Strutt turned the table on the *Aces*, heading home Maynard and his fellow ex-second halfer at Belle Vue, Maurice Payling, who had been dubbed 'Slant' by former *Aces* manager, Johnnie Hoskins, apparently not because of his riding style but because of the form of his handwriting.

Maynard and Payling, struggling against the home combination, were next to appear as a pairing for Belle Vue in heat 14. By that stage Norwich had established a sixteen point lead and the tie was on a knife edge.

With the exhortations of manager Ken Sharples, a former Belle Vue rider himself, and their team-mates ringing in their ears, Maynard and Payling lined up at the tapes alongside the same home duo that had given Norwich inspiration in heat four, Edwards and Strutt.

Maynard and Payling, in the words of a later tribute, gave the race everything they had, fighting for vital points at a crucial stage of the match. During the course of the

The camaraderie engendered by shared danger has probably contributed to the exceptional appetite of retired speedway riders for getting together to relive past glories. Sometimes the veterans take to the track once again and this picture from 1997 shows the former Poole riders who came together for a second half contest against a vintage Southampton side. L-r, Ross Gilbertson, Ken Mellor, Bill Holden (on the bike), Bobby Croombs, Pete Swain, Ted Laessing. Kneeling is Mike Vernam.

A get-together off the track for riders who have appeared for either Leicester and Long Eaton or, in several cases, for both teams. Standing, L-r, are Geoff Bouchard, Keith White, Vic White, Peter Wrathall, Norman Storer and Norman Hunter. Sitting, l-r, James Bond, John Boulger, Howard Cole and John Hart.

heat, the two collided, resulting in the death of Maynard and serious injury to Payling, who although he returned to the sport, was perhaps never again the same force.

After the loss of Maynard and Payling, Belle Vue's attempt to maintain the first leg lead understandably petered out, despite a brave attempt by Peter Craven to keep his side in the hunt. Ove Fundin completed an 18 point maximum score from his six rides, beating Peter Craven in the final heat, for which the competing riders were nominated.

The score over the two legs was tied at 107-107. At that period there was to be no toss of a coin or two-man race-off to decide the result. The semi-final would be re-ridden, again over a full two legs.

Meanwhile, at Stoke, Tony Robinson had enjoyed a good evening, inspiring his Sheffield *Tigers* to a win over the home team. It was in a good mood, somewhat tempered by an exchange with the *Potters'* co-promoter Mike Parker, that he returned to Stockport and went straight to bed. He was woken in the early hours by the police, with the news that Tink Maynard was dead and Slant Payling critically injured. Robinson remembers:

> It really knocked me sideways, particularly the thought that I was going to have
> to get into the car at some stage and drive north to break the news to Tink's mother.
> I just sat there, thinking, when there was another knock at the door. It was Peter
> Craven, back from Norwich, thinking he had to break the sad news to Mrs Maynard.
>   Peter sat with me for a while, trying to help me cope with the news, until he
> finally went home. It was a dreadful time, losing a friend.

The circumstances of the aftermath of Derek Maynard's death produced not one but two bitter ironies. Belle Vue and Norwich squared up again in the replayed semi-final of the National Trophy, with Norwich winning both legs, the second in Manchester by just one point, against an understandably subdued Belle Vue.

Taking Tink Maynard's place for the *Aces* in both legs was Tony Robinson, who recalls:

> You just have to get on with it if you are determined to remain in speedway. Tink was dedicated to speedway and he would have understood.

The second irony, in view of the fact that it was the much admired Peter Craven who had consoling words for Robinson immediately after his friend's death, is the fact that just three years later Craven, who had won a second World title in 1962, was killed at Old Meadowbank in Edinburgh, thrown into the safety fence after attempting to avoid a fallen home rider. Craven's Belle Vue partner in that race was Robinson's brother-in-law, Bill Powell.

Speedway has gradually developed much more sophisticated precautions against death or serious injury. Safety barriers, composed of sprung wire mesh, solid wooden boards, steel sheets or, in one exceptional case in the late 1920s, of piled turves, have been replaced at the top level by air fences. Lighting standards, in earlier times spaced at even intervals around the tracks, and on occasions struck by riders who had lost control of their machines, sometimes with fatal results, have often been replaced by much taller pylons or towers, well out of harm's reach.

Back protectors give riders just that little bit more security and each competitor today has a cord fitted to his handlebars which automatically cuts off engine power once released when a rider falls, reducing the risk of injury from moving parts such as the unguarded primary chain of the speedway machine. In many past incidents when the bike was still operation, riders were dragged for long distances along the track surface.

Speedway will continue to be a dangerous sport. But no matter whether the riders involved in a crash are from their own team, or the opposition, the fans care deeply about their welfare. Whatever the result of a match, the biggest cheer of a night can often be when a rider walks away from what looks initially like a bad crash, mounts his machine for a re-run of the race, ignores the shaking he has received as a minimum from his spill, and sets out once more to thrill the crowds.

Speedway riders can be extremely superstitious, and many have complicated rituals when it comes to donning their protective clothing or approaching the starting tapes. This rosette worn by fans supporting the Long Eaton *Archers* and depicting the team's teenage star Ray Wilson, later England's winning captain in the Speedway World Cup, would originally have been in the colours of green and yellow. They were changed to red and yellow after being deemed unlucky following a dreadful run of injuries during which Wilson himself broke a thigh in a crash at Weymouth.

WHEN SPEEDWAY WAS FUN

Coronation Street star Pat Phoenix (Elsie Tanner) is introduced by Stoke promoter Reg Fearman to his riders, l-r Bill Wainwright, Pete Jarman, Colin Pratt and Ken Adams.

Birmingham has always been renowned for its metal bashing industries. The *Brummies* riders seem to be taking it literally as Eric Boothroyd (right) wields a hammer on Harry Bastable's machine.

A *Brummie* symphony. The riders take to the bandstand at a supporters' social event. Pictured left to right are Alan Pearce, Harry Bastable, Dan Forsberg and Eric Boothroyd, while team manager Phil Hart is seated at the drums.

Out of the forest. Long Eaton *Archers* supporters club secretary George Wood and his son Georgie don their Robin Hood-style outfits to spend a Sunday afternoon at Rye House.

Many speedway pits areas today are totally shut off from public gaze. Sheffield in the early 1960s encouraged audience participation, as supporters enjoy watching Tony Robinson prepare his machine for the evening's racing.

Supporters give a helping hand at Rye House by buying much-appreciated new tyres for Clive Hitch, Roy Trigg and Eric Hockaday. Such presentations were commonplace and indicate the close relationship in speedway between riders and fans.

Not sure if this really is fun. John Hart puzzles out how to get his engine back in place.

How many young fans would have been delighted to take the place of this lucky mascot, on parade with Ken McKinlay for an international fixture.

Coventry promoter Charles Ochiltree (second left, talking into the microphone) believed in linking sport to the community. He encouraged Coventry fans to raise funds for guide dogs for the blind. This early 1960s shot includes Coventry riders Jack Biggs (third from left) and Ron Mountford.

(Left) Frolics on tour in the mid-1950s, in the then Union of South Africa. Ian Williams (left) and Reg Duval, spending the English winter racing on SA circuits, meet a member of a touring theatrical revue.

Dennis Newton, who raced and lived in South Africa, was one of several riders over the years to entertain crowds at the interval by singing over the track microphone. Howdy Byford and Len Silver formed a double act at Exeter, and Eric Chitty of West Ham made commercial gramophone records after World War Two and performed in clubs.